About the Author, Richard L. Baxter

Dick was called by God on January 12, 1977 at 7:05 PM in Renton Washington after a friend he worked with invited him and his wife, Nina, to church. They went to get him off his back.

Not wanting to go, Dick got very drunk beforehand so he wouldn't care where he was. After the preacher, who was full of love and the joy of God did 5 minutes of announcements, Dick was crying. Fifteen minutes later God had wrapped His loving arms around him and delivered him from alcohol, drugs, smoking, theft, and hate. Then God placed a call to preach on his life and gave him a knowledge of the Word in his heart, (he could quote you scriptures and didn't own a Bible). The next day He and Nina started sharing the Word with people and leading them to the Lord.

Over the next two and a half years, at work they lead about 55 people to the Lord. Four of which went into full time ministry.

They interned as a pastor to a new singles' church in Seattle. In one year the church grew to about 150 people. They were associate pastors in Spokane, Washington, where they helped with the bus ministry. In one year it grew from a hand full of kids to 5 buses loaded up.

As a youth pastor in Wapato, Washington they led many young people to the Lord and grew to a point that they were out growing the main body. A number of those young people are still involved in full time ministry.

As senior pastor in Ahtanum, Washington they started a new church and held a minimum of 3 services a week for 5 years. They never held a service where at least one soul was brought to the Lord. To this day scores of those souls are pastoring and ministering to the lost.

Currently their ministry is supporting churches and new pastors with council and training.

Ministering to the people of the world today has become a challenge to most of us. In writing this short booklet, the goal is to keep it simple and help pastors to overcome the many frustrations in growing the body of Christ. They pray that this simple, basic, original plan will help polish the armor of God that they put on years ago.

This book is dedicated to all the wonderful people God has allowed us to share the simple truth of His powerful word. Through growth and discipleship you have brought thousands of new souls to the kingdom of God. Our hearts are filled with many memories of the loved ones we have prayed with, stood with, protected, cared for, and even sent them home to Jesus. With tears in my eyes even as I pin this note, I pray that God may bless each and everyone of our spiritual children and grandchildren.

DISCIPLESHIP AND MORE

2 Timothy 2:2

AND THE THINGS YOU HAVE HEARD ME SAY
IN THE PRESENCE OF MANY WITNESSES,
ENTRUST TO RELIABLE MEN WHO WILL BE
QUALIFIED TO TEACH OTHERS

GOD'S WILL IS THAT
ALL MEN BE SAVED.

JESUS DIED SO THAT
MAN COULD BE SAVED.

THE HOLY SPIRIT IS HERE SO THAT
MAN CAN BE SAVED.

MAKING CHURCH GROWTH
A LIFESTYLE

If God would speak just one word to us to-day, it might be…..

DISCIPLESHIP

In Ecclesiastes 1:9, it says, "….There is nothing new under the sun." Some times we just need a simple reminder to be on track with the Master Teacher, being Jesus Himself. He always had a definite plan in His mind. He was not won-dering about what to do next to make His plan work out. He just didn't tell people what was going on, or share the fine points of His plan. He went about this plan in His daily activities of ministry. He talked with people, sharing Gods love, building relationships, meeting the needs of His fellow man, and always looking for the ones who seem to hang around Him the most.

There were many people over the course of two and a half years, (of His three years) of ministry, that would follow Him, talk with Him, serve Him, and ask questions of Him. They would see and hear amazing things and miracles they had never seen before. Yet they would come and go. Some even said, "Lord I will follow you wherever you go." In Luke 9:58, "Jesus replied, "Foxes have holes and birds of the air have nests, but the Son of Man has no place to lay his head." Jesus even called a few men out to follow Him. Mark 1:17, "Come, follow me," Jesus said, "and I will make you fishers of men." All of this walking from town to town had a wonderful purpose. The last two and a half years or so of hard work, was about to pay off. His plan was about to take shape. The entire world was about to have the most amazing change happen to it that had ever taken place before. The organization of the church, the foundation for the growth within the Kingdom of God was about to take the stage. Jesus was ready to share part of His secret plan with a handful of men, who had no idea what was going to happen in their future.

This is a major scripture and the base to truly understand growth.   Mark   3:13-19,   "[13] Jesus went up on a mountainside and called to him those he wanted, and they came to him. ¹⁴ He appointed twelve-designating them apostles-*that they might be with him* and that he might send them out to preach ¹⁵ and to have authority to drive out demons. ¹⁶ These are the twelve he appointed: Simon (to whom he gave the name Peter), ¹⁷ James son of Zebedee and his brother John (to them he gave the name Boanerges, which means "sons of thunder"), ¹⁸ Andrew, Philip, Bartholomew, Matthew, Thomas, James son of Alphaeus, Thaddaeus, Simon the Zealot ¹⁹ and Judas Iscariot, who betrayed him."

Let's get a grip on this one. Jesus had probably walked with most of these men for a couple of years by now. The testing ground was, who came to more teachings, walks, potlucks, and so forth. Also, who was willing to serve, take orders, and run some errands. These men were the ones. I really don't think that there was a bolt of lightning from heaven telling Jesus to pick certain men out of a crowd. There were a lot of men to choose from. Jesus could have built a glass cathedral and put some gold angles around the pulpit, and taken a big offering. You might note none of that was in His plan. His goal was to change the world, and He knew that you can only change the world as you change one man at a time. Jesus needed to find reliable men, who had proved themselves to be capable of receiving His plan for changing the world. These men were the ones that showed the greatest interest in what Jesus was doing.

He could have chosen 50 men that day. I will share more on this later. I will say this, have you ever tried to take 50 Boy Scouts on a camp out? They all have knives, hatchets, and fishing poles with sharp hooks. You are all by yourself. Let me know how that worked out for you.

What Jesus did is He called 12 men to Him, that He had noted as trustworthy. Next, He gave them an official title. You are my Apostles. They were probably feeling pretty good about now. This is the start of where you and I came from. Jesus just organized the ground work for church growth. This is the true pattern for a church growth model that Jesus used. The model that Jesus the master teacher set up will work as good today as it did 2000 years ago. It is simple and natural and it flows with life itself. Souls are won into the Kingdom and people are trained up and needs are met.

Taking care of the church, or the People in the Body of Christ, was the job of many men and women. Not just **one**. The structure that was set in place was a Godly design that needs to be followed. Ephesians 4:11-12, "[11] It was he who gave some to be apostles, and some to be prophets, and some to be evangelists, and some to be pastors and teachers, [12] to prepare God's people for works of service, so that the body of Christ may be built up." It tells us that He gave us different gifts but it is all to prepare God's people for works of service. We are in a people processing business that takes organization and cooperation from many. The question is, who are you appointing to watch over, a hand full of saints?

Mark 3:14, **THAT THEY MIGHT BE WITH HIM...** is the most important thing in the verse. He had called these reliable men to be at His side, so that true teaching could take place. Discipleship 101. This was not about preaching on Sunday morning, or being in charge of Sunday School. No, this was that you will learn the mysteries of the kingdom of God. Jesus was willing to share his heart with these men to the point that the entire church was going to be left in their hands. This is the changing point for all of mankind, the birth of the first church of this world. Not only that, but how the Church should operate from inside out, not from outside in. Jesus did not hire people to help from a long distance, he raised up people from within.

You might note here, that Jesus was not looking for people with letters in front of their names or ordination papers hanging on their walls. He was looking for people that would follow Him in love.

I was at a Bill Gothard Jr. meeting with about 1200 licensed, or ordained ministers for 3 days. On the last day Bill asked the question, "How many of you know that God has really called you into ministry?" About 100 men raised their hands.

You need to note here that Jesus spent much time searching for men who would be trustworthy and reliable. He was testing these men over time and miles of His journey. These men had to learn the way of God's Holy Spirit. They were about to learn the mysteries that had been hidden for ages.

**You can't help people,
until you Disciple people to Disciple people.**

The Apostles were confused about this, and asked Jesus a question. In Matthew 13:10-13, "[10] The disciples came to him and asked, "Why do you speak to the people in parables?" [11] He replied, "The knowledge of the secrets of the kingdom of heaven has been given to you, but not to them. [12] Whoever has will be given more, and he will have an abundance. Whoever does not have, even what he has will be taken from them. [13] This is why I speak to them in parables: "Though seeing, they do not see; though hearing, they do not hear or understand."

Jesus knew that you can only help so many people at a time. He had picked His hand full and was dedicated to helping them, and the rest would have to wait. The 12 were about to train the 72, and the 72 were about to train the 500, and the 500 were about to train the 3000. Just a math note here, no one was responsible for more that about 6 people here, about half of what the Master Teacher was doing.

Jesus was not about numbers, but He was

after committed believers. He was more interested in winning 100% of you, and you winning 100% of the world. He was way more focused on **Discipleship than Pulpit Ministry**. By Him giving His secret wisdom to the Sunday crowd, was like throwing your pearls to the pigs. He was more interested in finding those who were willing to sell all they had to buy the fine pearl. Matthew 13:45-46, 45 "Again, the kingdom of heaven is like a merchant looking for fine pearls. 46 When he found one of great value, he went away and sold everything he had and bought it".

You also have to make a note here. You can only have so many relationships at one time. Jesus was human like you and me. There is only 24 hours in a day. Between work, family, and rest time, we are limited to just a few relationships. We need to be honest with ourselves, and realize that we are not Superman. If the Master Teacher taught 12, and one of those slipped away, I believe that the scripture in Matthew applies to us here. Matthew 10:24 "A student is not above his teacher, nor a servant above his master." It is enough for a student to be like his teacher, and a servant like his master.

The mysteries that Jesus would refer to would be the ability to hear the Holy Spirit of God

The mysteries that Jesus would refer to would be the ability to hear the Holy Spirit of God in their lives and be humble and yield to the call and the will of the Lord in their lives. The next thing is that Jesus would send these men out to share the Word with others because the fields were white unto harvest. Matthew 9:35-38, "[35] Jesus went through all the towns and villages, teaching in their synagogues, preaching the good news of the kingdom and healing every disease and sickness. [36] When he saw the crowds, he had compassion on them, because they were harassed and helpless, like sheep without a shepherd. [37] Then he said to his disciples, "The harvest is plentiful but the workers are few. [38] Ask the Lord of the harvest, therefore, to send out workers into his harvest field.""

A heart beat for souls comes with the Holy Spirit. When we accept Him as Lord of our life, it comes as a package deal. If we don't have this, we don't have Jesus either. Sharing Christ is like breathing to a disciple. It is a driving force for us and the compassion that the Lord has for the lost. To help them is to find one more reliable disciple to help carry the cross and the burden we share.

This is the mind set of a disciple. 1 Timothy 4:16, "Watch your life and doctrine closely. Persevere in them, because if you do, you will save both yourself and your hearers." Being conscience of your life's actions, words, and thoughts, is what walking in the Spirit is about.

In the Great Commission, Jesus said to go and make Disciples, to get them baptized and to teach them to do what you're doing. Which part of this are we not getting a grip on? There are many people who come to a church building, but not many who are the church. This is why pulpit ministry should not be our focus all the time. Many want a savior, but not a new Lord. There is a major difference to this thought process. When the people don't have the need to share Christ with everybody, it's because they want a Savior, but the Lordship of Christ could be at a distance. This is where Jesus taught us that foxes have holes.

Discipleship is taught from the inside out, not from the outside in.

We simply assist the Holy Spirit, by being an example and being obedient, to the Lordship of Christ. As Paul said in 1 Corinthians 11:1 "Follow my example as I follow the example of Christ."

TRAVELING ON THE ROAD

As an evangelist, who traveled for a number of years, I was in a new or different church every week.

I prayed with pastors all over this country. Many were frustrated about church growth. My first question to them was, how many men are you discipling? The usual answer was, I have 7 families in my church, or I have 14 families and two single men in my church. That's great I'd say, but how many of those men do you disciple? The pastor would say, well they all show up on Sunday. That's great I'd say, but how many of those men do you disciple? Preaching is not DISCIPLING.

Here's a problem. If we have never been a disciple, how do we disciple?

First, we have to spend a lot of time with Matthew, Mark, Luke and John. This approach is to wear out your Bible by reading the 4 Gospels.

Then do what Jesus did; discipleship gives opportunity for disciples to disciple other. This is done at work, home, sports, and other avenues. We are the salt and light, bloom where you are planted.

Let's keep this simple. I have found that if I just share Jesus with everybody I meet, some will come back and say, what do you mean by that? This gives me the opening to answer their questions, build a relationship and become a model for them to follow as we spend time together. As their relationship grows with the Lord and I continue to answer their questions. They grow to the point where the Lord is feeding them and unity takes place. Unity means he is coming into maturity. I start to sense the gifts and calls that the Lord has gifted them with and start to send them out into ministry with blessing. By this the church is added to. I want you to note that this is all done in a personal way, not from a pulpit.

I need to add something here that I really believe is very important. In today's church scene people come to church and set in pews or chairs for an hour or two and then leave. We call this fellowship at church as we stare at the back of someone's head during this time. I want to make a suggestion here to help a discipleship lifestyle. There needs to be time for our disciple leaders to talk with and build relationships with not only new people, but touch base with those they are overseeing. Circle moments, coffee moments, prayer or updates of news of some event could be shared. This is like a family time moment. Remember it's all about building relationships. Love God, neighbor and self. It's about practicing the growth of the Spiritual Fruit in your life. People talking, caring and sharing.

In a church my wife and I pastored, we had the Youth Group do lunch every Sunday. They were asked to set up the tables with games and puzzles. People would stay after church for 2 or 3 hours every Sunday. Lunch was not a troublesome thing, but an easy lunch for a small cost. The leaders would talk to new people and invite them to a table. All the people would love on them the rest of the afternoon. We saw people come to the Lord every week. It was like the largest family I've ever had.

IMITATIONS

There has been and will be many attempts to manufacture some kind of Church growth

Many will include our tradition of pulpit ministry, professional music or fancy buildings. None of these will match the pattern model that Jesus set for us to follow. I John 2:6, "Whoever claims to live in him must walk as Jesus did." Preaching from a pulpit has a special place in the kingdom of God, and it's always good to hear wonderful music, over poor music, and going into a clean, nice, warm building is better than sitting on a wet blanket. We all understand this. But with the mixture of our world and the church and the flashing lights, the standards for soul winning have been lowered some. This is not my real topic here so I want to be very brief.

Jesus looked for reliable men, men He could count on. Paul said the same thing to Timothy. 2 Timothy 2:2, "And the things you have heard me say in the presence of many witnesses entrust to reliable men who will also be qualified to teach others". Reliable men, that's the key here.

Note… if it take a rock music group to win them, it will take a rock group to keep them. If it takes a fired up preacher to get them, it will take a fired up preacher to keep them. This is not some game that Jesus was playing. It was a war whether people live or die without a savior. He gave His life to prove this.

There has also been several attempts to manufacture a form of discipleship.

A. SHEPARDING… YOU FOLLOW ME, I'll tell you how to act, what to do, what to read and what to listen to. This is the heavy handed father image. Keep your eyes on me type of leader. Note here that Jesus takes second place to this leader. I know everything, so you must always come to me for the answers.

B. GIFT PROJECTION… All Christians should be just like me. This leader is blinded to other gifts within the body. You must be just like him or your wrong. His grace and mercy are all wrapped up in his little gifting. You feel guilty in your walk with Christ, because you can't live like this leader.

C. CULTS… I have the secret, God/Angel has spoken to me. The blood of Jesus was not enough to give me salvation, so I must do more for my sins.

D. PROGRAMS… The major replacement to discipleship. The Church has adopted this in place of the true structure that was given to us from heaven. This is milk toast, when the church needs a hearty meal of meat.

E. LEGALISTIC… do's and don't, my way or the hi way.

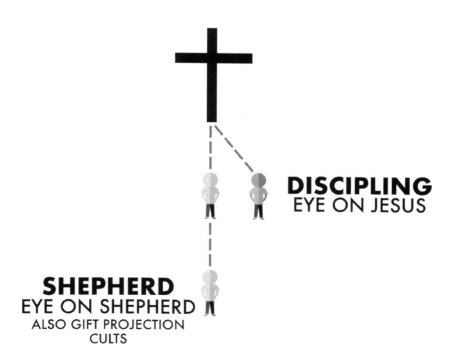

DISCIPLING
EYE ON JESUS

SHEPHERD
EYE ON SHEPHERD
ALSO GIFT PROJECTION
CULTS

Just a few nuggets Jesus knew that you can only change the world, as you change one man at a time. You can only change a man as you pour your life into them over time.

Discipleship is not a program… It is a life time commitment of sharing and building relationships.

IT IS A LIFESTYLE

That which is built with love and time will last. As we are looking for a worthy person to share discipleship with, it will require that you are the Bible. Lots of people know the Bible and many Bible stories. They have gone to church since World War One. Still they have no idea how to be the Bible.

If people who go to a church are holding on to the ways of the world, in debt, not developing Fruit of the Spirit in their home and life, are unable to communicate in a loving family way, then they are not ready to disciple. They might be ready to be discipled, if, I say if, they voluntarily submit themselves to be taught.

Let's say this couple submits to be trained up. You have built a relationship over things that interest both of you. Hiking, fishing, and watching sports. This is what I call common ground. It's a natural place for you to do the work of the Lord. Being the Bible means that when you go hiking, your being a Bible. An example of how you're full of joy, and concerned about his welfare. You can be a servant and set up the tents and so forth. Pray over the meals. Share a simple experience, where God intervened in the situation. Answer his questions with a love and respect for his life. And apply spiritual training to situations of actual life.

Discipleship is about being with them and sharing. This could include a football game, a night out to dinner, round of golf, or birthday party. The key is being with them. Let's say it takes a year to bring a person to maturity. That makes two of you or two families that are sold out to Jesus.

The next year both of you find a worthy person to share with, doing the things you enjoy doing. Another year goes by and now there are 4 families involved. The next year, 8 families will be moving with Jesus. In 4 years 16 families. 5 year's 32 families. 6 year's 64 families. 7 year's 128 families. 8 year's 256 families. 9 year's 512 families. In 10 years 1024 families. This is not a perfect world, so these numbers could shift around a bit.

> WE NEED TO HAVE
> MORE DRIVE BY FRUITINGS.

God wants us to enjoy and have an abundant

life.   Sharing the love of Jesus with people should be our joy. It should be like the oxygen we breath.

A person needs to show interest in the spiritual things before you can work with them. Stop trying to push a noodle up hill and find someone interested. If you always have to go to them, they are not eager enough to learn yet. Jesus's disciples followed Him.

HOW DO WE REALLY BUILD RELATIONSHIPS?

Answer… By allowing God's Holy Spirit to work through us to bear His fruit, so that a starving world can eat of this Godly Fruit and taste the goodness of Jesus Christ our Lord.

I have people ask me all the time, what I'm I supposed to do in the Lord? Surrender to Jesus and develop the Fruit is my answer. Our only work in the Lord is to develop the Fruit of the Spirit. Let's take a minute and think about that.

> OUR ONLY WORK IN THE LORD
> IS TO DEVELOP
> THE FRUIT OF THE SPIRIT!

The fruit is the center of God's will to win souls for His Kingdom. I am not crazy, but I am simple. I believe in KISS. Keep It Simple Sweetheart.

I call this the great exchange. Jesus takes away the bad and fills us with the good. Now that is a great exchange. It's found in Galatians 5:19-25, "[19] The acts of the sinful nature are obvious: sexual immorality, impurity and debauchery; [20] idolatry and witchcraft; hatred, discord, jealousy, fits of rage, selfish ambition, dissensions, factions [21] and envy; drunkenness, orgies, and the like. I warn you, as I did before, that those who live like this will not inherit the kingdom of God. [22] But the fruit of the Spirit is love, joy, peace, patience, kindness, goodness, faithfulness, [23] gentleness and self-control. Against such things there is no law. [24] Those who belong to Christ Jesus have crucified the sinful nature with its passions and desires. [25] Since we live by the Spirit, let us keep in step with the Spirit."

If you are taking notes here, you'll note that everything in the sinful nature is designed to destroy relationships. Everything in the Fruit of the Spirit is designed to build relationships.

In John 10:10 "The thief comes only to steal and kill and destroy;" (note the sinful nature here) "I have come that they may have life, and have it to the full." (note the fruit here). Also in Jesus words in Matthew 22:37-40 "[37] Jesus replied: "Love the Lord your God with all your heart and with all your soul and with all your mind. [38] This is the first and greatest commandment. [39] And the second is like it: Love your neighbor as yourself. [40] All the Law and the Prophets hang on these two commandments". The first and second commandments are all involved in the Fruit of the Spirit.

All that we do in Christ revolves around building relationships. This is true worship of Christ. 1 John 2:6 "Whoever claims to live in him must walk as Jesus did." Jesus was full of the fruit, and we need to be like Him, in our actions, thoughts and attitudes. Philippians 2:5 "Your attitude should be the same as that of Jesus Christ." The Fruit of the Spirit only starts to grow after a born again experience. Remember, that the Fruit is Spiritual Fruit, that only comes from God. That's when our Spirit meshes with the Holy Spirit and together we become one. This only happens when the Holy Spirit knocks on the door of our heart and we allow Him into our life and repent of our sins and declare Jesus Christ to be the Lord of our life. Romans 10:9-10 [9] "If you confess with your mouth, "Jesus is Lord," and believe in your heart that God raised him from the dead, you will be saved. [10] For it is with your heart that you believe and are justified, and it is with your mouth that you confess and are saved".

To have the best life possible on this earth, it is like the song, Jesus take the wheel. He will give us driving directions and guidance to stay on the path of His grace and mercy.

I want to clarify about spiritual fruit. Some

might say that their friend was a loving, friendly, kind person who would give you the shirt off their back. Although, they lived a life separate from Jesus. I would say that the devil is a deceiver and a cheap imitation of what is right, and he is committed to steal people away from the truth. The word says in Proverbs 12:10, "....The kindest acts of the wicked are cruel.

That God shaped hole in our heart that just got filled by the Holy Spirit is an eternal type place. I like to call it the **present tense** place. As humans, we live by time and date, a **time zone** place. Our bodies may live 50, 70, 90 years or so. But our spirits were given form at the beginning of time. Our spirits will still be here after our body turns to dust. God lives in the **present tense**. Hebrews 13:8, "Jesus Christ is the same yesterday and today and forever." Also in 2 Peter 3:8 "But do not forget this one thing, dear friends: With the Lord a day is like a thousand years, and a thousand years are like a day."

Our spirit and God's Spirit live in the **present tense place**. God's Spirit is the ONLY thing that can fill the **present tense** hole in our life. Many people have tried to fill that hole with sex, drugs and rock n` roll, but it will never work. Those are time zone temporary things that will all perish. Only **present tense** can heal the **present tense**. I will add that the Fruit of the Spirit is also in the present tense. This fruit that is in us, due to the work of the Holy Spirit within, is the Godly spiritual fruit that feeds and attracts the starving and hungry, worldly person to the drawing and attention of God, for the salvation of their souls. That God shaped hole in man's heart is craving for the Love that only comes from the *Heavenly fruit of present tense love.*

That love was made official 2000 years ago, when Jesus stretched out His arms and said, I love you this much. This is an *eternal present tense love.*

We now carry that cross in the form of the fruit of Love, by dying to self, and allowing the Spirit to use us in the Heartbeat of God's ever present Master Plan. His Will.

His Love still supersedes all things. Our work is to develop that spiritual fruit. The fruit is the ever present life of Christ in action today and every day. It is the essence of God's will in motion.

We are the only Bible that most people will read. Inside of them, (those controlled and lied to by the enemy) is that starving God shaped hole that they have a yearning to feed and fill. The junk that they have been feeding that present tense place does not satisfy their hunger. The junk they have been feeding on is all time zone garbage. It is nothing more than like a bandage placed over cancer, and then lied to and told that they will be OK. No, they need Present Tense Living Fruit to eat, to satisfy their hunger and fill that God shaped hole.

We need to completely understand this and be the Bible. Don't just read the Bible or just go to church, be the Bible because you are the church. Carrying the cross is all about being the church.

In Luke 14:27, Jesus told us to carry the cross and follow Him. If you don't, you are not His disciple.

What does He mean? The cross for us today means we surrender to His Lordship and die to ourselves. We let Him live through us as we grow with in the spiritual fruit, which lives in the present tense.

When we are reaching out to the world and the Holy Spirit can touch them through His fruit, miracles take place. Ungodly hearts can turn into Godly hearts.

Carrying the cross is the spiritual fruit and the heartbeat of God's will for souls, souls, souls.

A NUGGET OF MYSTERY TRUTH

Jesus told us to pick up the cross and carry it. The cross represents death and sacrifice and new life. John 12:24, "I tell you the truth, unless a kernel of wheat falls to the ground and dies, it remains only a single seed. But if it dies, it produces many seeds".

The mysteries of us carrying the cross, is that every person we interact with through the day may be hungry for the meal of love we carry in us.

The book *Death To Self*, is about water Baptism and a confession of the Lordship of Christ in your life. Not salvation, but Lordship. We either have to be under the Lordship of Satan, or Christ. Our focus has to be directly on the risen Lord. Our love of the Lord has to be a pure Love, and a direct connection. If not, our understanding of God's plan is at best, seen through a fog or a smoke filled lens. Romans 12:1-2, "Therefore, I urge you, brothers, in view of God's mercy, to offer your bodies as living sacrifices, holy and pleasing to

God—this is your spiritual act of worship. [2] Do not conform any longer to the pattern of this world, but be transformed by the renewing of your mind. Then you will be able to test and approve what God's will is—his good, pleasing and perfect will."

Again, God's will is that souls come to Him, through the work of the spiritual fruit by the Holy Spirit in our lives. His good, pleasing and perfect will is only tested and proven by us developing this Godly Fruit and seeing that souls are won to Him.

When we're busy doing God's Will, it's interesting to note that is when prayers are answered and many spiritual gifts and miracles take place, besides a lot of growth in the family of God.

THE EFFECTS OF
GOOD FRUIT STATEMENT!

The Fruit of the Spirit comes from God, but the effects of the Fruit of the Spirit are shown to people through relationships. It's all about building relationships for the Kingdom of God.

This sums it up nicely. Colossians 3:1-17, "[1]Since, then, you have been raised with Christ, set your hearts on things above, where Christ is, seated at the right hand of God. [2]Set your minds on things above, not on earthly things. [3]For you died, and your life is now hidden with Christ in God. [4]When Christ, who is your life, appears, then you also will appear with him in glory. [5]Put to death, therefore, whatever belongs to your earthly nature: sexual immorality, impurity, lust, evil desires and greed, which is idolatry. [6]Because of these, the wrath of God is coming.

[7] You used to walk in these ways, in the life you once lived. [8] But now you must rid yourselves of all such things as these: anger, rage, malice, slander, and filthy language from your lips. [9] Do not lie to each other, since you have taken off your old self with its practices [10] and have put on the new self, which is being renewed in knowledge in the image of its Creator. [11] Here there is no Greek or Jew, circumcised or uncircumcised, barbarian, Scythian, slave or free, but Christ is all, and is in all. [12] Therefore, as God's chosen people, holy and dearly loved, clothe yourselves with compassion, kindness, humility, gentleness and patience. [13] Bear with each other and forgive whatever grievance you may have against one another. Forgive as the Lord forgave you. [14] And over all these virtues put on love, which binds them all together in perfect unity. [15] Let the peace of Christ rule in your hearts, since as members of one body you were called to peace. And be thankful. [16] Let the message of Christ dwell in you richly as you teach and admonish one another with all wisdom and as you sing psalms, hymns, and spiritual songs with gratitude in your hearts to God. [17] And whatever you do, whether in word or deed, do it all in the name of the Lord Jesus, giving thanks to God the Father through him."

This round of scripture is a great example of the GREAT EXCHANGE. That is to accept Christ as Lord, and rid yourself of the worldly fruit that destroys relationships. Then taking on a personal experience of gaining relationship with the Lord, by putting on the armor, or clothing of the Spirit to build relationships for the Kingdom of God. Building relationships and discipling requires Godly fruit, not cars, houses, or bank accounts.

Romans 7:5, "For when we were controlled by the sinful nature, the sinful passions aroused by the law were at work in our bodies, so that we bore fruit for death".

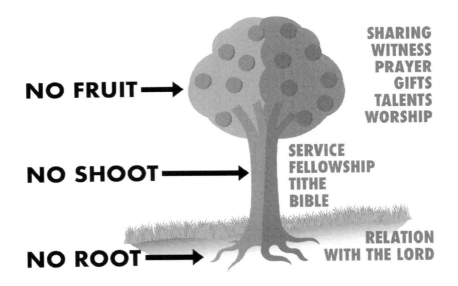

NO FRUIT → **SHARING WITNESS PRAYER GIFTS TALENTS WORSHIP**

NO SHOOT → **SERVICE FELLOWSHIP TITHE BIBLE**

NO ROOT → **RELATION WITH THE LORD**

CLEANING THE HOUSE

Let me give a helping hand on a subject here. Many times people can stumble due to simple misunderstanding. Let me start with this scripture.

2 Timothy 2:20-21, "[20] In a large house there are articles not only of gold and silver, but also of wood and clay; some are for noble purposes and some for ignoble. [21] If a man cleanses himself from the latter, he will be an instruments for noble purposes, made holy, useful to the Master and prepared to do any good work."

There are 3 houses to deal with. Church house, your house, and your body's house. This scripture tells us that IF we clean them up, so to speak, then God can use us. Let me add a tough love scripture to the mix here. 1 John 2:15-17, "[15] Do not love the world or anything in the world. If anyone loves the world, the love of the Father is not in him. [16] For everything in the world—the craving of sinful man, the lust of the eyes, and the boasting of what he has and does—comes not from the Father but from the world. [17] The world and its desires pass away, the man who does the will of God lives forever."

What I'm getting to here, is that if our houses need to be sanctified for the Lord, they need to be set apart from the world. If we are to cleanse our heart for the Lord, then the home we live in needs to be a holy place also.

While traveling as an Evangelist, I had a reputation as the Fire Bug. I would preach this message about the third night of a revival, to cleanse your home. The next night people would bring items from their home to burn in the parking lot. A small church of 80 people would bring enough stuff to fill 6 pickup loads to burn.

We lose blessings in our life when we allow sin in our life. Our families suffer if we allow sin to enter our home.

Philippians 4:8 "Finally, brothers, whatever is true, whatever is noble, whatever is right, whatever is pure, whatever is lovely, whatever is admirable—if anything is excellent or praiseworthy—think about such things."

Hebrews 3:1 "Therefore, holy brothers, who share in the heavenly calling, fix your thoughts on Jesus, the apostle and high priest whom we confess."

WE REALLY NEED TO GROW OR WE DIE.

2 Peter 1:3-11, "³ His divine power has given us everything we need for life and godliness through our knowledge of him who called us by his own glory and goodness. ⁴ Through these he has given us his very great and precious promises, so that through them you may participate in the divine nature and escape the corruption in the world caused by evil desires. ⁵ For this very reason, make every effort to add to your faith goodness; and to goodness, knowledge; ⁶ and to knowledge, self-control; and to self-control, perseverance; and to perseverance, godliness; ⁷ and to godliness, brotherly kindness; and to brotherly kindness, love. ⁸ For if you possess these qualities in increasing measure, they will keep you from being ineffective and unproductive in your knowledge of our Lord Jesus Christ. ⁹ But if anyone does not have them, he is nearsighted and blind, and has forgotten that he has been cleansed from his past sins. ¹⁰ Therefore, my brothers, be all the more eager to make your calling and election sure. For if you do these

things, you will never fall, [11] and you will receive a rich welcome into the eternal kingdom of our Lord and Savior Jesus Christ".

Pastoral ministry is great, but will never take the place of personal growth. Going to your home church, and hearing fifty-two sermons a year is great, but it can have a tendency to stunt your personal growth. Personal growth comes from personal relationship with Jesus Christ our Lord. The best sermon in the world is still only milk at best. You cannot preach meat, it is not possible. Some may argue with this teaching, but this is my story and I'm sticking to it.

Did you know sheep live in rich grasses fields, and eat that vegetation all the time, but it will kill them. Sheep need protein to live. Sheep require fiber to ensure proper function of the first stomach, (the rumen), a modified part of the stomach wherein bacteria digest cellulose from the plant into usable nutrients like protein. Rumination permits this vegetation to be chewed on later. They need peace and a quiet place to ruminate. Healthy sheep will spend a third of their life, ruminating, which is belching up a ball of grass from the stomach, chewing it and then swallowing it. I think that is interesting. The bacteria chemical is their key to life.

We have a similar challenge. We drink in this milk, with some nutrients in it, and feel all warm and fuzzy. The problem is, we can't live on milk alone. In 1 Peter 2:1-3, "[1]Therefore, rid yourselves of all malice and all deceit, hypocrisy, envy, and slander of every kind. [2] Like newborn babies, crave pure spiritual milk, so that by it you may grow up in your salvation, [3] now that you have tasted that the Lord is good."

We get this milk in us and then we go home and chew on it some more, and talk about it, and think about it, and then start applying it in our life. That's when the miracle takes place. The Holy Spirit is the chemical inside us that turns the milk into meat.

Hebrews 5:13-14, "[13]Anyone who lives on milk, being still an infant, is not acquainted with the teaching about righteousness. [14] But solid food is for the mature, who by constant use have trained themselves to distinguish good from evil."

The Key, is not that we just hear the Bible. But we become the Bible.

WE MIGHT BE THE ONLY BIBLE
SOME PEOPLE MAY READ.

James 1:22-25, "[22]Do not merely listen to the word, and so deceive yourselves. Do what it says. [23] Anyone who listens to the Word but does not do what it says is like a man who looks at his face in a mirror [24] and, after looking at himself, goes away and immediately forgets what he looks like. [25] But the man who looks intently into the perfect law that gives freedom, and continues to do this, not forgetting what he has heard, but doing it—he will be blessed in what he does.

Matthew 7:24-27, "[24]Therefore everyone who hears these words of mine and puts them into practice is like a wise man who built his house on the rock. [25] The rain came down, the streams rose, and the winds blew and beat against that house; yet it did not fall, because it had its foundation on the rock .[26] But everyone who hears these words of mine and does not put them into practice is like a foolish man who built his house on sand. [27] The rain came down, the streams rose, and the winds blew and beat against that house, and it fell with a great crash."

It's all about personal relationship, with Jesus Christ. Learning about Jesus is a life long pursuit. It's the joy of our lives. It is the command of God Himself. That is that we Love! Matthew 22:37-40, Jesus replied: "'[37]Love the Lord your God with all your heart and with all your soul and with all your mind.' [38] This is the first and greatest command-ment. [39] And the second is like it: 'Love your neigh-bor as yourself.' [40] All the Law and the Prophets hang on these two commandments."

When we forget this, we forget the real cost of the price paid by Jesus Christ.

I READ
THE HOLY SPIRIT VERSION
OF THE BIBLE!

Let me add some basic training here. I've heard several people have serious fights over which bible you are suppose to be reading. Our Bible is the best, because yours is missing this or that word. Right? This is ignorance in the face of the Almighty God. I know the Word because I have read the Bible quite a few times in the last 40 some years. You should remember that Christians did not have a Bible to read for almost 1800 years, due to no printing presses. So how did that all work out you ask?

Look at 1 John 2:27, "As for you, the anointing you received from him remains in you, and you do not need anyone to teach you. But as his anointing teaches you about all things and as that anointing is real, not counterfeit–just as it has taught you, remain in him."

I also know what it says in 2 Timothy 3:16–17, "16All Scripture is God-breathed and is useful for teaching, rebuking, correcting and training in righteousness, [17] so that the man of God may be thoroughly equipped for every good work."

2 Peter 1: 20-21, "[20]Above all, you must understand that no prophecy of Scripture came about by the prophet's own interpretation. [21] For prophecy never had its origin in the will of man, but men spoke from God as they were carried along by the Holy Spirit."

God, also in His wisdom, did an amazing things for us. He entrusted the Holy Spirit with all the truth of God's Word to teach us in a personal way. Now that is amazing. So what is interesting here is that whichever version you are reading, the Holy Spirit, which lives in us believers, will bring you the truth of the Word in a heart beat. As you read the Word, that man has put down on paper with all of his great intelligence of Greek and Hebrew, into English, Spanish, French, and whatever the other 1500 different languages are, excuse me but which version did you say was the only one that Paul read, and it's good enough for me.

The Word is so important that God trusted man to a certain point, because He does know our hearts, that He actually trusted the truth of God's Word to the Holy Spirit. Like I said before, 1 John 2:27.

1 Corinthians 2:12-13, "[12]We have not received the spirit of the world, but the Spirit who is from God, that we may understand what God has freely given us. [13] This is what we speak, not in

words taught us by human wisdom but in words taught by the Spirit, expressing spiritual truths in spiritual words."

James 1:21, "Therefore, get rid of all moral filth and the evil that is so prevalent and humbly accept the word planted in you, which can save you."

Here is a serious nugget of truth. Christianity is the only true religion that does not have to be taught, but only accepted. All other religions need to train you in their rules.

WE REALLY NEED TO GROW
OR YOU DIE

Not only do we have the Holy Spirit within us, but Jesus also did an amazing thing to all mankind. He made a new covenant for us all. Prior to the cross and His death the old covenant was in place. (The Ten Commandments on stone, which had to be read out loud to the people.) While in the tomb, heavenly work was taking place. One, Jesus took the keys of death away from Satan. Revelation 1:18, "I am the Living One; I was dead, and behold I am alive for ever and ever! And I hold the keys of death and Hades." Two, He went into holding cells of the wicked and righteous who had already died and preached to the dead.

1 Peter 4:6, "For this is the reason the gospel was preached even to those who are now dead, so that they might be judged according to men in regard to the body, but live according to God in regard to the spirit."

Roman 5:13, "For before the law was given, sin was in the world." But sin is not taken into account when there is no law." Also Roman 14:9, "For this very reason, Christ died and returned to life so that he might be the Lord of both the dead and the living."

And 3, He took the hard copy of stone copy away and put the word in everybody's heart and mind instantly.

In Hebrews 8:10-11, "[10]This is the covenant I will make with the house of Israel after that time, declares the Lord. I will put my laws in their minds and write them on their hearts. I will be their God, and they will be my people. [11] No longer will a man teach his neighbor, or a man his brother, saying, 'Know the Lord,' because they will all know me, from the least of them to the greatest."

Is this great or what? We are a walking Bible. The Word is in our minds already and it's in our hearts. And now being tied into the Holy Spirit, within us, we can understand God's Word because The Holy Spirit is the truth of the Word. Titus 2:11-14, "[11]For the grace of God that brings salvation has appeared to all men. [12] It teaches us to say "No" to ungodliness and worldly passions, and to live self-controlled, upright and godly lives in this present age, [13] while we wait for the blessed hope— the glorious appearing of our great God and Savior, Jesus Christ, [14] who gave himself for us to redeem us from all wickedness and to purify for himself a people that are his very own, eager to do what is good."   Also, in 2 Peter 1:3-9, "[3]His divine power has given us everything we need for life and godliness through our knowledge of him who called us by his own glory and goodness. [4] Through these he has given us his very great and precious promises, so that through them you may participate in the divine nature and escape the corruption in the world caused by evil desires. [5] For this very reason, make every effort to add to your faith goodness; and to goodness, knowledge; [6] and to knowledge, self-control; and to self-control, perseverance; and to perseverance, godliness; [7] and to godliness, brotherly kindness; and to brotherly kindness, love. [8] For if you possess these qualities in increasing measure, they will keep you from being ineffective and unproductive in your knowledge of our Lord Jesus Christ. [9] But if anyone does not have them, he is nearsighted and blind, and has forgotten that he has been cleansed from his past sins."

God's word is also a secret language. It is only known to those with the true born again experience. 1 Corinthians 2:14, "The man without the spirit does not accept the things that come from the spirit of God, for they are foolishness to him, and He cannot understand them, because they are spiritually discerned".

I had a bracelet made for myself, with an engraving on it. It has the letters WWJD, etched into it. When it comes to understanding the Word of God, and you need answers for life, WWJD is the best prayer you can ask. WHAT WOULD JESUS

DO?

I will add this to the subject. What is written on our heart is not James 3:4 or 1 Peter 5 :7. What is written is that the presents of God the Creator is real. That good and evil are with us, and that's where we get our laws from, rights and wrongs, and our desire to Worship and praise.

SATAN'S LARGEST WEAPON

The desire to praise something. Religion is his greatest tool. Religion will make people hijack airplanes, kidnap people, and fly into tall buildings. It was the religious people who crucified Christ. Religion is nothing more than a bandage put over cancer to cure it.

People have a great desire to follow something. They like form and ritual. It's a God given desire. That God shaped hole in our hearts that needs to be satisfied. Satan has used this to the max. It is his master plan to draw souls away from Christ.

Religion is not Christian. Religion is the LIE from the pits of hell. Sex, drugs, and rock-n-roll don't even come close to satan's master plan of religion. There are many religions, but only one leader for them all, and that's the devil.

Christianity stands alone by the blood of Christ.

THE WORD OF GOD IS SIMPLE

Let's not lose track here. I'm still talking about Discipleship, the Word, and the office of the Holy Spirit.

Our goals in life are to build Disciples, train newbies in the Word, and show them how to be used best by the Holy Spirit, so that they can have a blessed life.

Let's talk on God's Word for a few seconds. It's simple….. It's super simple!!

Jesus told us how simple it really is in Matthew 22:37-40, "Jesus replied: "Love the Lord your God with all your heart and with all your soul and with all your mind. [38] This is the first and greatest commandment. [39] And the second is like it: 'Love your neighbor as yourself. [40] All the Law and the Prophets hang on these two commandments." Basically, if you can master these simple three things (I might add will only take the rest of your life), you got it made. Our entire work in the Lord, as a believer is all wrapped up in a nut shell in these three simple things to do. Love God, love your Neighbor, and love yourself.

Nothing in the Word goes past these three commands. There is no law. Try if you will to add or subtract from this. It can't be done. Test any scripture in the Word against these three commands and you will come up empty.

The three Commands of love God, love your neighbor, and love yourself, are basic life goals.

6 BASICS OF THE NEW TESTAMENT

Then Paul throws in six other basic teachings to get a grip on. These are in Hebrews 6:1-2, "[1]Therefore let us leave the elementary teachings about Christ and go on to maturity, not laying again the foundation of repentance from acts that lead to death, and of faith in God, [2] instruction about baptisms, the laying on of hands, the resurrection of the dead, and eternal judgment."

Let me give you a quick explanation of these six teachings. You must remember that there were no bibles in print during this time, that's why God made the bible easy to follow and understand.

1. SIN.....Anything in rebellion to serving the Lord. OR I have my plans God and you have Your plans, let's just keep it that way. This is max rebellion. I'm smarter than you are God, and I don't need you to tell me how to do anything. By the products of maximum rebellion are the acts of the sinful nature.

2. FAITH.......Your dependence on God. Your complete trust in God.

3. BAPTISMS IN WATER.....

      A. 1 Peter 3:21, "And this water symbolizes baptism that now saves you also-not the removal of dirt from the body but the pledge of a good conscience towards God". People lost their head or their family right after their baptism in those days. A confession of Christ was a big deal.

      B. HOLY SPIRIT..... Acts 1:4-5, "[4]On one occasion while he was eating with them, he gave them this command: "Do not leave Jerusalem, but wait for the gift my Father promised, which you have heard me speak about. [5]For John baptized with water, but in a few days you will be baptized with the Holy Spirit"." Jesus wanted them to wait in Jerusalem until they had been clothed with power from on High, by the Holy Spirit.

      4. LAYING ON OF HANDS....this is the recognition of authority and submission to it. This is the authority, power, and structure that was used within the Church. Gifts come from God, and it is our responsibility to recognize what God has done to a disciple and be blessed by it. Hebrews 13:17, "Obey your leaders and submit to their authority. They keep watch over you as men who must give an account. Obey them so that their work will be a joy, not a burden, for that would be of no advantage to you."

      5. RESURRECTION OF THE DEAD… This is our HOPE. The ANCHOR for our soul.

      6. ETERNAL JUDGEMENT....This is our wit-

ness to the world, to prick their spirit to the life of Christ.

We also have the teaching of the Holy Spirit that lives within us, and this coupled with the Heartbeat of God as your driving force, you are a walking, talking New Testament Bible. This New Testament Bible is willing to shed the world, grow fruit, and carry out the Great Commission.

TREE OF LIFE

This tree of life is a simple way to show the growth in a disciple's life. In the limb on the left are the first three basics, of sin, faith, and baptisms. These are more related to the 1st Commandment and to God.

Basically, all sin is against God, our faith is only in God, and our confession of Lordship. The three on the right limb, laying on of hands, resurrection of the dead, and eternal judgment, are more related to the 2nd command. This is the authority, power, and structure we use within the church, this is our Hope, and this is our call to awaken people to real life.

The Nourishing life of the Holy Spirit flows through the body of this tree and gives it life. By our searching out and loving the Lord, the Fruit will grow and souls are brought to the Lord. This also shows how the **will** of God is accomplished.

TREE OF LIFE
WHAT YOU SOW IS WHAT YOU REAP
FRUIT OF THE SPIRIT, OF SOULS, OF LIFE

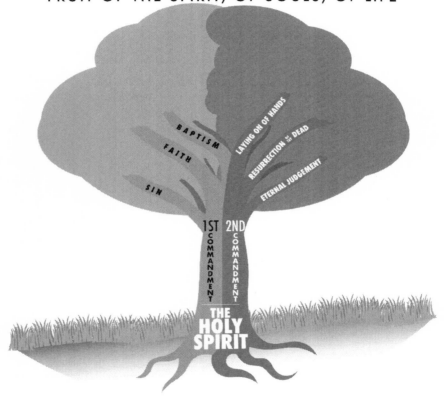

PROVERBS 11:30
THE FRUIT OF THE RIGHTEOUS IS A TREE OF LIFE,
AND HE WHO WINS SOULS IS WISE

THE SPEAR HEAD THAT IS THE DRIVING FORCE TO LIFE IN CHRIST

If you are looking for the Spearhead that drives all that Jesus called us to do, it is in the last words that Jesus gave His Disciples in Matthew 28:16-20, "[16]Then the eleven disciples went to Galilee, to the mountain where Jesus had told them to go. [17] When they saw him, they worshiped him; but some doubted. [18] Then Jesus came to them and said, "All authority in heaven and on earth has been given to me. [19] Therefore GO and MAKE DISCIPLES of all nations, BAPTIZING them in the name of the Father and of the Son and of the Holy Spirit, [20] and teaching them to obey everything I have commanded you. And surely I am with you always, to the very end of the age."

The Spearhead is to
Go, Disciple, Baptize,
and Teach His Commands.

THE HEARTBEAT OR GOD'S WILL

GOD'S WILL IS THAT
ALL MEN BE SAVED.

JESUS DIED SO THAT
MAN COULD BE SAVED.

THE HOLY SPIRIT IS HERE SO THAT
MAN CAN BE SAVED.

When I said, "Lord, come into my heart", I got God's heartbeat. Now everybody I meet becomes a potential disciple of Jesus Christ.

This is the driving force of a true believer. The Heartbeats. Souls....souls....souls....souls.

The Holy Spirit brings God's master plan with Him along with the rest of His office supplies. The Holy Spirit is God and He comes directly from God, He sees the face of Jesus all the time, He is Jesus. God's will lives in the believer, feed it, love it, surrender to it, breathe it, share it, and glorify it with your life. My own heart races with this information to share with my readers, I have so much to share at this point, and wish I could just open my heart and let you see what God has given me. I can tell you that the Spirit yearns to be heard in these last days, because the fields are white unto harvest. Please send out more workers into the fields.

Understanding the will of God or the Heartbeat of God, changes our whole attitude about growth in the Lord. If every person we meet is a potential disciple for Christ, how do we act or respond knowing this information? What is our attitude in the presence of all the people we talk to? Am I showing the Fruit of the Spirit and the love of God during my transaction of life? How do I act at home, at work, in church, or at play? Do I set a good example to those around me at all times? Does my character represent the attributes of Christ?

I call this awareness of the Heartbeat of God our Spearhead for a major reason. When we do what Jesus said to do, Go, make disciples, baptize them, and train them. The word Go is the first Heartbeat. When we Go and share our testimony and God's love with another person, one of two things happen. They accept you and your God given message, or they reject you and your message.

One of two things now takes place inside of you when they reject you and God's love. One, you crumble and fall or give up. Two your heart is filled with compassion for this soul. It might be your spouse, or dad. You go away and fall on your knees and call out to God for them? God, what do I say to them, I don't want them to go to hell, I want them to go to heaven with me and You. You go to church and tell what happened and ask for prayer and help. You study the Word and look for that one verse that might make a difference to them.

Now what just happened? One, **Witness** due to the joy of the heartbeat. Two, **Prayer** and **Faith** in God to help you. Three, going to **Church** and true **Fellowship**, and Four, study the **Bible** to gain knowledge and feed yourself so that others can be helped. Now that is why I call the Heartbeat the Spearhead of our Faith.

Here is a serious question. How many people do you know that go to church and never go witness? How many people do you know that claim to read the Bible, but don't go to church? How many people do you know that go to church, but never pray? Going to church will not drive you to pray or witness. Praying and reading the Word will not drive you to fellowship or church. None of these are spearheads or heartbeats.

GOD'S WILL OR GOD'S DIRECTION FOR YOUR LIFE

God's will, or Heartbeat **is the same for all mankind.** Your direction in life will differ from one another, but God's Will is the same for everybody. You may miss your direction in life, by being a carpenter, when you should have been a doctor, but you still don't have to miss out on God's Will, because you can bloom wherever you are planted.

Believers need to understand this clearly, to save confusion in their minds and hearts. I have heard so many different slants to Gods Will, such as, was it God's will for my husband to die, or my baby to die? Some have said, isn't it God's will to heal all these sick people? I will tell you, if everything is good in your life, your faith is never challenged. 1 Peter 1:6-7, "[6]In this you greatly rejoice, though now for a little while you may have had to suffer grief in all kinds of trials. [7] These have come so that your faith—of greater worth than gold, which perishes even though refined by fire—may be proved genuine and may result in praise, glory and honor when Jesus Christ is revealed."

God's Will is simple and not going to change. It's all about the war of souls, and our allegiance to the Lordship of Christ, over the devil. Our direction in life is a place to do God's Will. We are to be the salt or the light wherever we go.

As I write this, just this week 17 young people were killed by another young person under the control of satan. He open fired on a school classroom, and sent 17 people to their eternity. I'm so sorry to say it is to late too pray for these 17 souls. All people are destined to die and then face the judgment. What really concerns me is were they under the Lordship of Christ or the devil? And did the Disciples share the faith with them in all the days before their death? Or was the salt and light company busy playing games and letting the Heartbeat of God set on a back burner?

OLD NUMBER 3

It's this Heartbeat that feeds our spiritual hunger for God, or I should say kick starts our Spiritual hunger, and our desire to continue to grow daily. It gives us true **purpose of life**, and delivers us from the lies of the devil, that tells us we are third class citizens. We can start to believe that we are fearfully and wonderfully made. Psalm 139:13-14, "[13]For you created my inmost being; you knit me together in my mother's womb. [14]I praise you because I am fearfully and wonderfully made; your works are wonderful, I know that full well."

A major problem for believers is old number 3. Love yourself. Number 1, loving God, and number 2, loving your neighbor, seem to be easier to accomplish. Having a grip on that Godly Heartbeat puts us back on a level playing field. We really start accepting the truth of God's Word over the lies of the devil, when the Heartbeat is in the right place. The Heartbeat helps us to separate light from dark, and truth from lies. 1 Peter 2:9, "But you are a chosen people, a royal priesthood, a holy nation, a people belonging to God, that you may declare the praises of him who called you out of darkness into his wonderful light.

By our declaring our love to Him in public, as a witness, we are elevated as a son or a daughter to the King of Kings. We no longer live in the lies of darkness, but now live in the Light of truth.

God's Word is truth. When He says we're fearfully and wonderfully made, we can take that Word home and put it in our bank and draw interest!!

THE OFFICE OF THE HOLY SPIRIT

Jesus promised us the Holy Spirit for our born again experience, as we accept the work of the cross, and the blood shed for our sins.

This is not the end of life as we know it. The Holy Spirit has His own office to work from. He comes bearing many gifts for our spiritual growth. All good things come from above.

Galatians 4:6, "Because you are sons, God sent the Spirit of his Son into our hearts, the Spirit who calls out, "Abba, Father.""

I am so glad that God did not leave us alone to fight the battles of the flesh. When we ask Jesus to come into our lives, he did by sending His Holy Spirit into our lives, to bond with us. The Holy Spirit is full of power and love. He is also super charged with reverence for God, hate for sin, and true humility. Humility to the point that He will never push you beyond free will. Now that is a serious point you have to think on. To love God and obey Him is a choice. God is not looking for puppets to serve Him, but people who love Him with their whole heart.

The Holy Spirit brings these gifts with Him and shares them. We will notice them quickly happening in our new life in Christ.

These attributes of God are all wrapped up in the Holy Spirit, that is now wrapped up inside of us.

As the Holy Spirit meshes with us these qualities seem to radiate within and start to become part of us. They are gentle, respectful, and sweet. They also tend to radiate from us to others. The scripture to understand this is in 2 Corinthians 2:15-16, "[15]For we are to God the aroma of Christ among those who are being saved and those who are perishing. [16] To the one we are the smell of death; to the other, the fragrance of life."

Many times over the years, while in a store or on the street, I have just known that the person I was next to was a Christian. Without any introduction, I would ask, where do you attend church? Every time the response was the same, Oh I go to so and so church. I could feel the Holy Spirit in them.

The Holy Spirit will bring these mantles or cloaks from His office and lay them on our spirit.

1. Attribute of Reverence for God and Jesus Christ. You will desire to praise them. To respect them.

2. Attribute of Repentance. Your desire to sin

will be overpowered by your desire to live a holy life in Christ, and to please Him.

3. Attribute of Humility. You will bow down to God and His love and Word. The fight of your opinion will die, and your thinking will start to match up with God's heart.

Disclaimer… don't forget your free will can overpower anything God can try to help you with.

This is only a start of the gifts, talents, and abilities He will share with you from His office. We are all unique within the body of Christ. Each one is given shades of power, ability, talent, and skills. We each use whatever we have been given to glorify God in our daily life. 1 Thessalonians 4:11-12, "[11]Make it your ambition to lead a quiet life, to mind your own business and to work with your hands, just as we told you, [12] so that your daily life may win the respect of outsiders and so that you will not be dependent on anybody." Also Colossians 3:23, "Whatever you do, work at it with all your heart, as working for the Lord, not for men."

There is more to the Office of the Holy Spirit to come. What's important to know is that He is always working in us to improve our life and accomplish God's will at the same time. Proverbs 4:18, "The path of the righteous is like the first gleam of dawn, shining ever brighter till the full light of day."

ABOUT THE GIFTS

Let's just list these gifts first.

Called Gifts

Ephesians 4:11
Apostle
Prophets
Evangelists
Pastors
Teachers

Market Place Gifts

1 Corinthians 12:7-10
Wisdom
Knowledge
Faith
Healing
Miraculous Powers
Prophecy
Distinguishing between Spirits
Tongues
Interpretation of Tongues

Nature Gifts

Romans 12:6-8
Prophesying
Serving
Teaching
Encouraging
Giving
Leadership
Mercy

God in His wisdom calls people to the Five Fold Ministry. These are church builders, overseers, and leaders within the body of local churches. Generally, they are the paid staff and taken care of by the body, because they give their full time to work for the Lord in His House.

The Market Place Gifts are in complete control by God's hand only. 1 Corinthians 12:11, "All these are the work of one and the same Spirit, and He gives them to each one, just as He determines." Also, they are given for the good of many people to see. In other words, they are for the Market place. If we are in tune with the Lord, He will use us in any of these gifts at any time.

The Nature Gifts we are born with. I believe that they can really come to life within, after a born again experience. These gifts can all be used to help in the advancement of the Body of Christ.

Maybe you know your gifts, and maybe you don't. I think it is good to explore the gifts and learn about them. The thing is, don't get frustrated about them at all. Why do I talk like this you ask? Because God's Will to love supersedes all the above.

1 Corinthians 13:1-8, 13, "¹If I speak in the tongues of men and of angels, but have not love, I am only a resounding gong or a clanging cymbal. ² If I have the gift of prophecy and can fathom all mysteries and all knowledge, and if I have a faith that can move mountains, but have not love, I am nothing. ³ If I give all I possess to the poor and surrender my body to the flames, but have not love, I gain nothing. ⁴ Love is patient, love is kind. It does not envy, it does not boast, it is not proud. ⁵ It is not rude, it is not self-seeking, it is not easily angered, it keeps no record of wrongs. ⁶ Love does not delight in evil but rejoices with the truth. ⁷ It always protects, always trusts, always hopes, always perseveres. ⁸ Love never fails…. ¹³ And now these three remain: faith, hope and love. But the greatest of these is love."

All the gifts are designed for the purpose of God's will, that is to bring people to Christ. Developing the fruit of love is the best gift of all. The commands to love God, neighbor and self, are the master keys to a full life in the Lord.

YOUR SPIRITUAL FREE WILL

Question? When does this really happen? Here is what I see in life and scripture. Your free will does not start until you have two choices to choose from. In 2 Corinthians 4:4, "The god of this age has blinded the minds of unbelievers, so that they cannot see the light of the gospel of the glory of Christ, who is the image of God." This means that there is only one choice here. Not much free will, wouldn't you say? It's kind of like when Moses is read. 2 Corinthians 3:15-16, "[15]Even this day when Moses is read, a veil covers their hearts. [16] But whenever anyone turns to the Lord, the veil is taken away."

When Jesus knocks on the door of our heart, and we let Him in, the scales fall off our eyes, and then we can see Him as He is, just like Paul could see. Now that we have seen the devil and we have seen Jesus, who do we want to serve? This is two choices now. That is spiritual free will. Jesus does not have puppets, He has a family that chooses to love Him with all their heart. If we chose sin over Jesus, so be it. That is spiritual free will choice.

In the world, people make lots of choices. They are not spiritual choices. They are just choices. They may be choices of right and wrong, or even what we call good or evil. These are still not spiritual choices. If you are already in sin or a worldly person living your life, and you die without Christ in your life, you're heading for Hell. In God's sight, Proverbs 12:10, ".....the kindest acts of the wicked are cruel". Proverbs 15:8-9, "[8]The Lord detest the sacrifice of the wicked,....."[9]The Lord detests the way of the wicked". Proverbs 15:26, "The Lord detests the thoughts of the wicked."

Let's call this a cloud of thought for a second. Stay with me. People have an inner desire to worship something. We know it is God given. Then satan comes along with a major history of tricks and lies, that he has accumulated over centuries of time to blind and confuse, and deceive people. This is the spiritual war we live in.

Why is this you ask? Romans 1:18-20, "[18]The wrath of God is being revealed from heaven against all the godlessness and wickedness of men who suppress the truth by their wickedness, [19] since what may be known about God is plain to them, because God has made it plain to them. [20] For since the creation of the world God's invisible qualities–his eternal power and divine nature–have been clearly seen, being understood from what has been made, so that men are without excuse."

Here lies the problem. The worldly people have rejected God who they have not seen from the inside out, of their life. In other words, they have not been born again, where Christ lives on the inside of us.

They have not tasted that the Lord is good. 1 Peter 2:2-3, "[2]Like newborn babies, crave pure spiritual milk, so that by it you may grow up in your salvation, [3] now that you have tasted that the Lord is good."

If they have never tasted this goodness from the inside out, how many choices are they really left with? When it comes to a spiritual freewill choice, I need two options to choose from, not just one.

If you have lived on both sides of this fence,

these last few paragraphs make it easy to get a grip on. I know your asking the question, ya but, ya, but? Wait a minute, don't we all have a freewill to choose or reject Christ? In the over all plan of God the answer is absolutely **Yes.** Jesus died so that man can come to Him when the Holy Spirit knocks on his heart' and the person lets Him in.

Kind of a final thought here is that free will is still about two choices. We are living in the last days, where deception and lies are blinding those that need Christ. We are cities on the hill that are lit up so that the blind can see and choose the truth of Jesus Christ to worship. The truth will set you free. John 8:32 B.

And again, God does not want puppets to serve Him, but desires that our freewill choice is in full swing, and full of love to desire Him.

A NEW DIAPER PLEASE

It's your turn to change the diaper this time, honey.

The question comes up, how long do Newbies intend to stay in diapers? People come to church year after year, hearing sermon after sermon. Yet you hear stories repeated, time and time again, where there is still fighting and divorce, rebellion, financial problems, drinking, drugs, and ungodly attitudes.

Let me clarify something here. The difference between Salvation and Lordship. First, Lordship. There are only two kingdoms talked about in this world. God's and satan's. God is the Lord of the Eternal Kingdom, and satan the lord of the earth. We are either under the Lordship of God or satan. If you are under the Lordship of God your reward is the salvation of your soul. We are actually saved when we go through Heaven's gates.

1 Peter 1:3-9, "³Praise be to the God and Father of our Lord Jesus Christ! In his great mercy he has given us new birth into a living hope

through the resurrection of Jesus Christ from the dead, [4] and into an inheritance that can never perish, spoil or fade–**kept in heaven for you**, [5] who through faith are shielded by God's power until **the coming of the salvation that is ready to be revealed in the last time**. [6] In this you greatly rejoice, though now for a little while you may have had to suffer grief in all kinds of trials. [7] These have come so that your faith–of greater worth than gold, which perishes even though refined by fire–may be proved genuine and may result in praise, glory and honor when Jesus Christ is revealed. [8] Though you have not seen him, you love him; and even though you do not see him now, you believe in him and are filled with an inexpressible and glorious joy, [9] for you are receiving the **goal of your faith**, **the salvation of your souls**."

Philippians 2:12-13, "[12]Therefore, my dear friends, as you have always obeyed–not only in my presence, but now much more in my absence–continue to work out your salvation with fear and trembling, [13] for it is God who works in you to will and to act according to his good purpose."

It's Lordship we really deal with on earth. People were just Disciples learning about Jesus, and then when they caught on and realized that Jesus could be and must be their Lord, they surrendered and made a public confession of the new Lordship of Christ in their life. We call this water baptism. In those days, declaring The Lordship of Christ, could have cost them their life.

We train many disciples, that may never except Christ as Lord. Jesus did, why can't we? Churches are full of them today. John 6:66, "From this time many of his disciples turned back and no longer followed him."

Many people want salvation, but the Lordship of Christ will cost them their life. 1 Peter 2:24, "He himself bore our sins in his body on the tree, so that we might die to sins and live for righteousness..."

Paul faced this question in Hebrews. He had had enough of this fighting and bickering among the church folks. The heartbeat of God was strong in Paul, and he let it loose on the church that day. Listen to his words to a church that was using super large over size diapers.

Hebrew 5:11-14, "[11]We have much to say about this, but it is hard to explain because you are **slow to learn**. [12] In fact, though by this time **you ought to be teachers**, you need someone to teach you the elementary truths of God's word all over again. You need milk, not solid food! [13] Anyone who lives on milk, being still an infant, **is not acquainted with the teaching about righteousness**. [14] But solid food is for the mature, who by constant use **have trained themselves** to distinguish good from evil."

In verse 13 is where about ALL the church problems come from. "Anyone who lives on milk, being still an infant, is not acquainted with the teachings about righteousness." (go back to page

46 and look at that sheep thing again, please.) Note, they have not died to sin yet and placed Jesus over their heart as Lord of their life. They are still just wanting salvation and a way to escape the consequences of Hell. They need to go back to grade school again, (the 7 basics) until they get a grip on Lordship. You will note, that you don't sense the attributes of the Holy Spirit about them. That is a spirit of reverence for God, a spirit of humility, or a spirit of repentance.

One of the problems we face every day is that we wake up alive. We need to pray every morning until we are dead to ourself. As Paul said, I die daily!

Pulpit ministry can only go so far. It can give you some milk, and teach you some basics. If discipleship is not in place to teach newbies how to fish on their own, you will only develop a maintenance church type group of people.

Paul went on to explain this in Hebrew 6:1-3, "[1]Therefore let us leave the elementary teachings about Christ and go on to maturity, not laying again the foundation of repentance from acts that lead to death, and of faith in God, [2] instruction about baptisms, the laying on of hands, the resurrection of the dead, and eternal judgment. [3] And God permitting, we will do so."

There are the basics that were taught in the early church. It does not take years to teach a hand full of basics. Once the training wheels are off, there are many roads to ride on. Can immaturity be cured? Can church problems be solved? The answer is, (drum roll please.) No and No! Not by man. Only by God. Jesus gave us the pattern of Discipleship and we need to follow it. We need to look through those church folks and see those that are interested in learning more.

Again, 2 Timothy 2:2, "And the things you have heard me say in the presence of many witnesses entrust to reliable men who will also be qualified to teach others."

Discipleship is like Jesus giving the blind man the second touch. Mark 8:22-25, "[22]They came to Bethsaida, and some people brought a blind man and begged Jesus to touch him. [23] He took the blind man by the hand and led him outside the village. When he had spit on the man's eyes and put his hands on him, Jesus asked, "Do you see anything?" [24] He looked up and said, "I see people; they look like trees walking around." [25] Once more Jesus put his hands on the man's eyes. Then his eyes were opened, his sight was restored, and he saw everything clearly."

Pulpit ministry is more like the first touch. Discipleship is more like the second touch. Jesus hand picked men to be with him, to spend time with Him. We need to hand pick men to be with us, and spend time with us. There is always more caught than taught.

As a pastor, when I focused on a family or person and spent time with them, their growth in the Lord would flourish. Many meal times have been spent in developing disciples. For me, pulpit ministry is about 2 hours of a Sunday. Discipleship takes up all the rest of my waking hours.

Here's a reliable **_manmade_** Proverb. Book of mine chapter 9:1 When I see you pay more attention to Jesus in public, I will start paying more attention to you in private.

Finding those interested, is the seek and search plan of church growth. Those people who will saddle up next to you for coffee and learn the mysteries of Christ. Paul said it this way in Ephesians 3:2-5, "[2]Surely you have heard about the administration of God's grace that was given to me for you, [3] that is, the mystery made known to me by revelation, as I have already written briefly. [4] In reading this, then, you will be able to understand my insight into the mystery of Christ, [5] which was not made known to men in other generations as it has now been revealed by the Spirit to God's holy apostles and prophets."

This is why Jesus walked with people for a few years before choosing 12 men, to be with Him, and share the mysteries of the Heartbeat. He chose well, because we are still here today to talk about the mysteries.

I ask people sometimes, if you were the only Christian left on earth, what would the church look like in 10 years?

HOLY CLOTHING STORE, ARMOR BOY

It's all about God, and there is no way around it. God's will is for all to be saved, Jesus died so we could get saved, and now the Holy Spirit is living in us to carry on God's will. Babies do need taking care of, but they by nature should grow up. After some potty training and some education, it's time to go to work and live like an adult.

Part of adulthood is knowing how to dress yourself. Not only that, but learning how to become useful in the work field of life and to be productive, and responsible.

In the spiritual realm, it's the same. We need to learn how to dress ourselves, and to become useful in service to the Lord, and be productive and responsible. God has plans for us all. He says that some plow, some plant, and some water, and He will give an increase into His Kingdom. Ephesians 2:10, "For we are God's workmanship, created in Christ Jesus to do good works, which God prepared in advance for us to do."

Paul said it very well in Hebrews 5:13-14, "[13]Anyone who lives on milk, being still an infant, is not acquainted with the teaching about righteousness. [14] But solid food is for the mature, who by constant use have trained themselves to distinguish good from evil."

Teaching people to train themselves is a major key. Now we are talking DISCIPLESHIP. Jesus shared this in Mark 3, saying that **they might be with Him**. He needed to teach these men how to train themselves. He even told them to wait in Jerusalem until they received the Holy Spirit who would help them.

John 16:5-16, "[5]Now I am going to him who sent me, yet none of you asks me, 'Where are you going?' [6] Because I have said these things, you are filled with grief. [7] But I tell you the truth: It is for your good that I am going away. Unless I go away, the Counselor will not come to you; but if I go, I will send him to you. [8] When he comes, he will convict the world of guilt in regard to sin and righteousness and judgment: [9] in regard to sin, because men do not believe in me; [10] in regard to righteousness, because I am going to the Father, where you can see me no longer; [11] and in regard to judgment, because the prince of this world now stands condemned. [12] "I have much more to say to you, more than you can now bear. [13] But when he, the Spirit of truth, comes, he will guide you into all truth. He will not speak on his own; he will speak only what he hears, and he will tell you what is yet to come. [14] He will bring glory to me by taking from what is mine and making it known to you. [15] All that belongs to the Father is mine. That is why I said the Spirit will take from what is mine and make it known to you. [16] "In a little while you will see me no more, and then after a little while you will see me."

Feeding yourself is that remarkable ability to hear the Spirit of God within you and obey. This is what brings unity to the body and causes it to grow. Ephesians 4:3-6, "[3]Make every effort to keep the unity of the Spirit through the bond of peace. [4] There is one body and one Spirit—just as you were called to one hope when you were called— [5] one Lord, one faith, one baptism; [6] one God and Father of all, who is over all and through all and in all." Also, Romans 1:5, "Through him and for his name's sake, we received grace and apostleship to call people from among all the Gentiles to the obedience that comes from faith."

Your life takes on a definite change at this point. Now from the inside out your view of Christ takes on a more Christ like nature. Your SPIRITUAL WARDROBE becomes your new dress code.

You enter the dressing room in Ephesians 6:10-17, "[10]Finally, be strong in the Lord and in his mighty power. [11] Put on the full armor of God so that you can take your stand against the devil's schemes. [12] For our struggle is not against flesh and blood, but against the rulers, against the authorities, against the powers of this dark world and against the spiritual forces of evil in the heavenly realms. [13] Therefore put on the full armor of God, so that when the day of evil comes, you may be able to stand your ground, and after you have done everything, to stand. [14] Stand firm then, with the belt of truth buckled around your waist, with the breastplate of righteousness in place, [15] and with your feet fitted with the readiness that comes from the gospel of peace. [16] In addition to all this, take up the shield of faith, with which you can extinguish all the flaming arrows of the evil one. [17] Take the helmet of salvation and the sword of the Spirit, which is the word of God. [18] And pray in the Spirit on all occasions with all kinds of prayers and requests. With this in mind, be alert and always keep on praying for all the saints."

I can't find anywhere that it says to take this warrior's armor off. We are in a war of Life and Death, Heaven and Hell. Understanding of the Heartbeat keeps the armor from rusting.

HOLY CLOTHING STORE, ARMOR BOY CONTINUED

Then there is some must wear personal relation type summer and winter wear. It fits great for all occasions and they all come's in one size fits all.

Colossians 3:12-14, "[12]Therefore, as God's chosen people, holy and dearly loved, clothe yourselves with compassion, kindness, humility, gentleness and patience. [13] Bear with each other and forgive whatever grievances you may have against one another. Forgive as the Lord forgave you. [14] And over all these virtues put on love, which binds them all together in perfect unity."

It's always good to be a bright light, rather than a dimwit. Romans 13:12, "The night is nearly over; the day is almost here. So let us put aside the deeds of darkness and put on the armor of light."

This new style sparkles, compared to that old drab look you used to wear around.

Romans 13:14, "Rather, clothe yourselves with the Lord Jesus Christ, and do not think about how to gratify the desires of the sinful nature."

Galatians 3:27, "for all of you who were baptized into Christ have clothed yourselves with Christ." See what I mean, just look in that mirror.

Ephesians 4:24, "and to put on the new self, created to be like God in true righteousness and holiness."

Now this is our new electrified line of wear, it's flexible and goes with anything you do.

Luke 24:49, "I am going to send you what my Father has promised; but stay in the city until you have been clothed with power from on high."

It's always good to clean up after playing in the mud, and getting super dirty. Hosea 10:12, "Sow for yourselves righteousness, reap the fruit of unfailing love, and break up your un-plowed ground; for it is time to seek the Lord, until he comes-and showers righteousness on you."

We suggest that this cleaning business becomes a permanent part of your daily activities so that everyone around you notices a major difference in your lifestyle.

1 John 3:3, "Everyone who has this hope in him purifies himself, just as he is pure."

1 Peter 1:22, "Now that you have purified yourselves by obeying the truth so that you have sincere love for your brothers, love one another

deeply, from the heart."

We might add that there is also a perfume line that goes well with all the clothing mentioned in this dress rehearsal. It's free to all who apply to this global ad for *THE HOLY CLOTHING STORE. JESUS and the CROSS.*

2 Corinthians 2:15-16, "¹⁵For we are to God the aroma of Christ among those who are being saved and those who are perishing. ¹⁶ To the one we are the smell of death; to the other, the fragrance of life.

This is the Heavenly line of fresh clothing made just for you. When you put this line of clothing on your friends and especially your family will just Love the new design and want to know the Designers Name and how they can get in touch with Him, so that they too can have clothes like this.

They say that these clothes will make a whole new person out of you.

ANOTHER DRIVE BY FRUITING.

Back again to the Office of the Holy Spirit. He lives in us to help develop the relationship building, attitude changing, character enhancing, mind changing, heart lifting, and vision setting life-style. In the words of a red neck, the stuff that makes you more like Jesus.

Jesus never takes things away from us, that He does not replace with way better things. We lose our desire to sin, and grow hungry for the wonders of God.

Let's go over a little more detail about the Fruit of the Spirit. **The Fruit of the Spirit comes from God, but the effects of the Fruit of the Spirit is shown to man through relationships.** The Fruit we're talking about here is what feeds a starving world. Let's take a look at the world from a scriptural view. In 2 Timothy 3:1-9, "[1]But mark this: There will be terrible times in the last days. [2] People will be lovers of themselves, lovers of money, boastful, proud, abusive, disobedient to their parents, ungrateful, unholy, [3] without love, unforgiving, slanderous, without self-control, brutal, not lovers of the good, [4] treacherous, rash, conceited, lovers of pleasure rather than lovers of God– [5] having a form of godliness but denying its power. Have nothing to do with them. [6] They are the kind who worm their way into homes and gain control over weak-willed women, who are loaded down with sins and are swayed by all kinds of evil desires, [7] always learning but never able to acknowledge the truth. [8] Just as Jannes and Jambres opposed Moses, so also these men oppose the truth–men of depraved minds, who, as far as the faith is concerned, are rejected. [9] But they will not get very far because, as in the case of those men, their folly will be clear to everyone."

You might note here that people, of the world, are a little corrupt, and have trouble with building any kind of solid relationship, due to a number of trust issues. Lies and deceptions are a standard because the devil is their father. Christians on the other hand, are building relationships by the Fruit and the truth of God's love. 1 John 5:19, "We know that we are children of God, and that the whole world is under the control of the evil one."

People of the world are starving for the truth, the Fruit of God, that is ever growing in us. A couple of things happen as we yield to the Lord, and the Fruit starts to appear in our life. One is that our lives become more peaceful. Troubles that we used to have seem to disappear. Our relationships with our family and friends take on new meaning. We seem to not only enjoy work more, but start to receive, increases and promotions. Our knowledge of the Lord inspires us to reach out to new people.

The next thing is that others notice the change. The Jesus side of the family and friends are more excited about us. Our employers take note of our extra efforts. Tension in the home is becoming family friendly. The worldly folks are so confused and waiting to see how long you're going to last. They hope you don't fall, but are taking bets that you will, so they do not have to look Jesus in the face and make a decision to accept Him like you did.

As a maturing disciple, it is good to learn how to hear the voice of the Spirit. You can develop a 24/7 communication line with the Lord. I am very careful what I feed my heart and mind. Here is how Paul said this, Philippians 4:8, "Finally, brothers, whatever is true, whatever is noble, whatever is right, whatever is pure, whatever is lovely, whatever is admirable–if anything is excellent or praiseworthy–think about such things."

What we feed ourselves spiritually plays a big part in our growth. By our new nature in the Lord and our connection to the Holy Spirit our desire should be fed on nutrients that please the Lord. Ephesians 5:10, "Find out what pleases the Lord." Our music, TV, books, entertainment and input revolves around uplifting or more Godly Nature. Proverbs 4:23, "Above all else, guard your heart, for it is the wellspring of life."

The HEARTBEAT is the real key, in hearing the Lord's voice. I seem to always listen to the inner voice when I am around people. Jesus shares with me words to say to people along the way. Maybe it's because of the HEARTBEAT again and the desire to give the Gift Of Christ to others, and steal another soul away from satan.

The Holy Spirit is inside of us to help us with these new changes. These changes are all for our personality, and attitude. Philippians 2:5, "Your attitude should be the same as that of Christ Jesus."

BE PRUNED AND FRUITFUL

The exchange comes at a price. God takes the bad and gives us the good. He paid a big price so that we could have this fruit. Again the Fruit is for building **relationships**. The commands, Love God, love your neighbor, and love yourself. Are all about relationships. The heart beat of God, souls, soul, soul. It's all about relationships.

Everything in the Commands, everything in the Spearhead or Heartbeat, is all about relationships.

Our **major work** in the Lord as a Christian, is to develop the fruit, so that we can build relationships within and for the Kingdom of God. This is so cool, to see this all tie together, and so simple. The oxygen of the believer is the Heartbeat, souls, souls, souls. The spiritual blood of the believer is the work of the Spirit within us developing the Fruit and keeping us alive. It is pumping through our spiritual veins. Jesus is the vine, we are the branches. God is the gardener and prunes us to be more fruitful.

John 15:1-17, "[1]I am the true vine, and my Father is the gardener. [2] He cuts off every branch in me that bears no fruit, while every branch that does bear fruit he prunes so that it will be even more fruitful. [3] You are already clean because of the word I have spoken to you. [4] Remain in me, and I will remain in you. No branch can bear fruit by itself; it must remain in the vine. Neither can you bear fruit unless you remain in me. [5] "I am the vine; you are the branches. If a man remains in me and I in him, he will bear much fruit; apart from me you can do nothing. [6] If anyone does not remain in me, he is like a branch that is thrown away and withers; such branches are picked up, thrown into the fire and burned. [7] If you remain in me and my words remain in you, ask whatever you wish, and it will be given you. [8] This is to my Father's glory, that you bear much fruit, showing yourselves to be my disciples. [9] "As the Father has loved me, so have I loved you. Now remain in my love. [10] If you obey my commands, you will remain in my love, just as I have obeyed my Father's commands and remain in his love. [11] I have told you this so that my joy may be in you and that your joy may be complete. [12] My command is this: Love each other as I have loved you. [13] Greater love has no one than this, that he lay down his life for his friends. [14] You are my friends if you do what I command. [15] I no longer call you servants, because a servant does not know his master's business. Instead, I have called you friends, for everything that I learned from my Father I have made known to you. [16] You did not choose me, but I chose you and appointed you to go and bear fruit–fruit that will last. Then the Father will give you whatever you ask in my name. [17] This is my command: Love each other."

The command to love, (God, Neighbor, and Self) or the Fruit of love, supersedes any opinion you may be hanging onto, or any habit you cling to. Even the attitude you have been known for. The height of your love is the length of your body stretched out on the alter of the Lord, because you were willing to sacrifice your opinion, habit, and attitudes at the cross, and die to self for the sake of your desire to follow the Lord and His Commands.

I have shared with people many times, that the hardest place in the world to live a Christian life is in their own home. I tell them that if they can master the home, then they can master the world. Your home needs to become the sounding board for your relationship with the Lord.

Home is my place, no boss to tell me how to act, or what to do. I come home and shut that door, and now it's My Time. I do and live as I please. I listen to what I want, watch what I want to watch, live how I choose how to live. Ya baby, this is really me, what you see is what you get. You better not tell that preacher what I did, or said. Yes this is the place we need to master in the Lord first.

I kind of directed this thought process on the

mind set of the man. There are two reasons for this. One, I have no idea how women thinks, does anyone? Two. Men, by God's Word need to lead their family into spiritual truth, and set the example of how Christ loved the church. It is the man's responsibility to train his wife and family up in the Lord. He must set the example and be the leader. Scripture tells us in 1 Timothy 5:8, "If anyone does not provide for his relatives and especially for his immediate family, he has denied the faith and is worse than an unbeliever."

ANOTHER DRIVE BY FRUITING

Just a little on the home life and the reliable man. Ephesians 5:22-33, "[22]Wives, submit to your husbands as to the Lord. [23] For the husband is the head of the wife as Christ is the head of the church, his body, of which he is the Savior. [24] Now as the church submits to Christ, so also wives should submit to their husbands in everything. [25] Husbands, love your wives, just as Christ loved the church and gave himself up for her [26] to make her holy, cleansing her by the washing with water through the word, [27] and to present her to himself as a radiant church, without stain or wrinkle or any other blemish, but holy and blameless. [28] In this same way, husbands ought to love their wives as their own bodies. He who loves his wife loves himself. [29] After all, no one ever hated his own body, but he feeds and cares for it, just as Christ does the church– [30] for we are members of his body. [31] "For this reason a man will leave his father and mother and be united to his wife, and the two will become one flesh. [32] This is a profound mystery—but I am talking about Christ and the church. [33] However, each one of you also must love his wife as he loves himself, and the wife must respect her husband."

For the reliable men who will hear this message, it's time to man up and become the true Pastor of your little flock. There is no such thing as a kingdom, unless there is a king and a queen.

> When you treat your wife like a queen,
> she will respond by treating you like a king,
> then a kingdom of peace will
> reign in your little castle.

The greatest way and (only way) to grow this wonder Fruit within is to become humble. Praise the Lord for the Holy Spirit within, who brings us the attribute of humility, repentance, and reverence for God. Simply said, we need to yield to the gentle voice of the Spirit, when He shares with us to repent.

The question is, what is our greatest tool for growth in the Lord? Its' our mistakes, our faults, our worldly tactics at building relationships. To put this in redneck terms that I could understand easily God spoke to me like a lightning bolt from heaven one day. He said, "You my precious son are a bugger brain, just like the rest of your red neck buddies. You say and do dumb stuff that hurts your wife, family and friends. You are missing my fruit in many of your words and actions. If you will give that dumb stuff to me when I bring it to your attention, I promise to take it away and give you a little pruning and then fruit will appear where it was not before. This will help you for the next time, because a little reminder of my loving hand will pop up and give you a slap on the back of your pointed little head. Are you good with this my precious son? Now go tell your wife you are sorry you said that to her, because she did not deserve that, and then pray together."

Growing in the Lord is way more important than hanging onto our pride. When we make mistakes with our spouse, due to anger, frustration, guilt, lies, or whatever, we need to repent to God and our spouse.

When we go to the other room after the incident, still upset, the small tender voice of the Lord will speak to you.

Jesus….. "Yo bro, what ya just do?"

Your mind….. "nothing, she had it coming!"

Jesus….. "Bro ya'all blowing it here, she your women. She loves you, and you just yelled at her."

Your mind….. "ya man, but I was mad!"

Jesus….. "you were mad because?"

Your mind….. "My boss told me I have to work this weekend."

Jesus….. "so you took your mad out on your women!"

Your mind….. "man that was dumb. Lord, forgive me."

You….. "Honey can I talk to you again. I'm sorry for my words and actions I said to you. You did not deserve that at all. It was all my fault.

I just talked to Jesus and asked Him to forgive me. Will you pray with me also to be more fruitful and a better husband to my most wonderful wife. Amen."

Turning mistakes into stairways of growth is a major key to being fruitful and having a wonderful home life.

HOW IS DISCIPLESHIP GOING TO WORK TODAY?

I'm about to step on a few toes here, I'm sorry to say. Many of our spiritual schools today teach a lot of knowledge, but not much life. What I'm trying to say is that book learning is good to a point, but learning by doing with the help of the Holy Spirit is better. 1 Corinthians 8:1-2, "[1]We know that we all possess knowledge. Knowledge puffs up, but love builds up. [2] The man who thinks he knows something does not yet know as he ought to know. Besides, milk will only take us so far down the trail of growth."

We do our best as men of God to grow in God, and sometimes we get in the way of ourselves to improve on God's plan. The old saying of, we never did it that way before, is probably wrong. The question comes back to us, what did Jesus do?

Again, He was human like us and had the same amount of hours in a day as we do. You can only build so many relationships at a time. He made three close relationships with Peter, James, and John. The other nine disciples played a major part in His plan, and were close to Him.

He preached to 5000, He challenged 72 to serve Him, He built a base with 12, and called 3 to become great leaders. He set us an example, for us to follow. John 13:12-17, "[12]When he had finished washing their feet, he put on his clothes and returned to his place. "Do you understand what I have done for you?" he asked them. [13] "You call me 'Teacher' and 'Lord,' and rightly so, for that is what I am. [14] Now that I, your Lord and Teacher, have washed your feet, you also should wash one anther's feet. [15] I have set you an example that you should do as I have done for you. [16] I tell you the truth, no servant is greater than his master, nor is a messenger greater than the one who sent him. [17] Now that you know these things, you will be blessed if you do them."

We can implement the same things Jesus did inside the local church. Jesus preached to the 5000. So preach, but only after you have prayed and received a real message from the Lord. A living message can go a long way.

Challenge those that want to be challenged to go with you to the fair this year, or the parade, or the air show, or a concert to share the love of the Lord with the people there. The idea here is that when we see you pay more attention to Jesus in public, I'll start paying more attention to you in private.

Pull those few aside that have been challenged, and that are seeking the Lord, and start to share your heart with them, in private. Share the mysteries of discipleship to those that are worthy. 2 Timothy 2:2, "And the things you have heard me say in the presence of many witnesses entrust to reliable men who will also be qualified to teach others."

Within that group look for the leaders who will rise up and help take charge of advancing the Kingdom of God. You will spend the greatest amount of your time with these men. Mark 14:32-34, "[32]They went to a place called Gethsemane, and Jesus said to his disciples, "Sit here while I pray." [33] He took Peter, James and John along with him, and he began to be deeply distressed and troubled. [34] "My soul is overwhelmed with sorrow to the point of death," he said to them. "Stay here and keep watch."

By doing this discipline lifestyle, your church will take on a whole new look. Let me give you a definition of a Discipleship Church.

> It's an organized body of believer,
> moving together with one voice
> to win souls for Christ.

Churches today are dying off and closing the doors at a rapid rate. They are the maintenance churches. No real growth, almost no young people, and lots of funerals. They preach 52 different sermons a year, and host potlucks monthly. They have given up on discipleship, because it is a lot of work, and replaced it with more bible studies, to learn more milk stuff. Yet people are not really having needs met. They are in the habit of Sunday church, bible studies, good old boy potluck, and don't rock the boat or offend the old saints. Still fighting and immaturity are always being tended to. These are pulpit ministry churches.

Pastor's have been trained that this is how we do church. I'm the great one here and you are the sheep. I know how to do it all. This mentality has killed the Spirit in many a new Christian, and has frustrated them to no end. They need help they can't seem to get, and on the other hand people want to help, but are pushed aside. Many give up and go home feeling UN-satisfied, or find a growing church.

DISCIPLESHIP AND LEADERSHIP IS NOT NEW

Moses had the same issues as most pastors do today. Jethro, his father-in-law stepped in with a timely message to save the day. Exodus 18:13-27, "[13]The next day Moses took his seat to serve as judge for the people, and they stood around him from morning till evening. [14] When his father-in-law saw all that Moses was doing for the people, he said, "What is this you are doing for the people? Why do you alone sit as judge, while all these people stand around you from morning till evening?" [15] Moses answered him, "Because the people come to me to seek God's will. [16] Whenever they have a dispute, it is brought to me, and I decide between the parties and inform them of God's decrees and laws." [17] Moses' father-in-law replied, "What you are doing is not good. [18] You and these people who come to you will only wear yourselves out. The work is too heavy for you; you cannot handle it alone. [19] Listen now to me and I will give you some advice, and may God be with you. You must be the people's representative before God and bring their disputes to him. [20] Teach them the decrees and laws, and show them the way to live and the duties they are to perform. [21] But select capable men from all the people–men who fear God, trustworthy men who hate dishonest gain–and appoint them as officials over thousands, hundreds, fifties and tens. [22] Have them serve as judges for the people at all times, but have them bring every difficult case to you; the simple cases they can decide themselves. That will make your load lighter, because they will share it with you. [23] If you do this and God so commands, you will be able to stand the strain, and all these people will go home satisfied." [24] Moses listened to his father-in-law and did everything he said. [25] He chose capable men from all Israel and made them leaders of the people, officials over thousands, hundreds, fifties and tens. [26] They served as judges for the people at all times. The difficult cases they brought to Moses, but the simple ones they decided themselves. [27] Then Moses sent his father-in-law on his way, and Jethro returned to his own country."

It was never intended to be a one-man show

Jethro gave Moses a good rebuke to help him see that he was not the only one who had gifts and abilities, and a heart to see things done right. Jethro also saw how the people were getting frustrated and time was wasting away. He put those two personal challenges together along with the wisdom of God, and brought it to Moses.

Moses, He asked, "do you see all these people looking disgusted over here?" You can't possibly help all these people with what is going on in their lives. You are going to have a nervous breakdown. You look tired and confused and worn out. Listen to me. You need to find some good men to help you. Godly men. Men who are reliable and trustworthy. Let each man be responsible for 10 men or less. Listen to me. Take your most advanced leaders and put them over 1000 men. To do this they will be over only 10 men who are over 100 each. These 10 men will have only 2 men under them, because they will be helping more in the training. These 2 men will have 5 men under them with 10 men under them and so one.

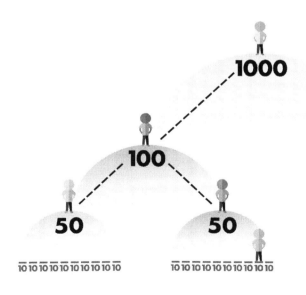

In this way all will be involved and feel useful, and all the people will have their needs met and go home satisfied. Do you get the idea Moses or do I need to go over this again. If you got it, I'm heading home to watch the latest donkey race on the net.

This plan that Jethro discussed with Moses came from God. Jesus is sharing the exact same plan with us. This plan works so well, that it is copied by ALL corporations, big and small business, the military, and industry of about every country.

It's called the structure of a business. Owners, managers, foreman's, lead man, worker. This is the simplified version. The structure is there to have organization, production and profit. It is understood by all. If you don't understand it, chances are you will get fired.

Question? Why does the church run like our Government? No order and no plan. We are suppose to have a plan... a major plan. We are in the people processing business. We are suppose to be an organized body of believers moving together with one voice to win souls for Christ.

How do we do this? The way Jesus did it, that's how.

THE JESUS PLAN
TO PREACH, TEACH & DISCIPLE

There is a difference between just pulpit ministry and discipleship. Let's continue to follow Jesus for a little while.

PREACHING

Matthew 4:23, "Jesus went throughout Galilee, teaching in their synagogues, preaching the good news of the kingdom, and healing every disease and sickness among the people." Matthew 9:35 is the same.

Mark 1:38, "Jesus replied, "Let us go somewhere else–to the nearby villages–so I can preach there also. That is why I have come."

Luke 4:43-44, "[43]But he said, "I must preach the good news of the kingdom of God to the other towns also, because that is why I was sent." [44] And he kept on preaching in the synagogues of Judea."

Luke 20:1, "One day as he was teaching the people in the temple courts and preaching the gospel, the chief priests and the teachers of the law, together with the elders, came up to him."

These 5 verses are all the same account of His walk.

NOTE: He preached a number of times, as was His custom, but take note there is nothing recorded about the sermon itself. Interesting!

JESUS TEACHING

Matthew 7:29, "because he taught as one who had authority, and not as their teachers of the law." Mark 1:22 the same.

Mark 4:2, "He taught them many things by parables, and in his teaching said:" Luke 5:3 the same.

Mark 10:1, "Jesus then left that place and went into the region of Judea and across the Jordan. Again crowds of people came to him, and as was his custom, he taught them."

Mark 11:17 "And as he taught them, he said, Is it not written:" 'My house will be called a house of prayer for all nations'? But you have made it 'a den of robbers."

Mark 12:35, "While Jesus was teaching in the temple courts, he asked, "How is it that the teachers of the law say that the Christ is the son of David?"

Luke 4:15, "He taught in their synagogues,

and everyone praised him."

John 18:20, "I have spoken openly to the world," Jesus replied. "I always taught in synagogues or at the temple, where all the Jews come together. I said nothing in secret."

Preaching 4 times, teaching 9 times a total of 13.

JESUS' PLAN TO DISCIPLE
He Chose them to be with Him

John 6:70, "Then Jesus replied, "Have I not chosen you, the Twelve? Yet one of you is a devil!"

Mark 3:20, "Then Jesus entered a house, and again a crowd gathered, so that he and his disciples were not even able to eat."

Mark 4:34, "He did not say anything to them without using a parable. But when he was alone with his own disciples, he explained everything."

Mark 6:1, "Jesus left there and went to his hometown, accompanied by his disciples."

Mark 8:10, "he got into the boat with his disciples and went to the region of Dalmanutha."

Mark 10:23, "Jesus looked around and said to his disciples, "How hard it is for the rich to enter the kingdom of God!"

Mark 11:11, "Jesus entered Jerusalem and went to the temple. He looked around at everything, but since it was already late, he went out to Bethany with the Twelve."

Luke 7:11, "Soon afterward, Jesus went to a town called Nain, and his disciples and a large crowd went along with him."

Luke 8:1, "After this, Jesus traveled about from one town and village to another, proclaiming the good news of the kingdom of God. The Twelve were with him."

Luke 12:41, "Peter asked, "Lord, are you telling this parable to us, or to everyone?"

John 1:39, "Come," he replied, "and you will see." So they went and saw where he was staying, and spent that day with him. It was about the tenth hour."

John 1:43, "The next day Jesus decided to leave for Galilee. Finding Philip, he said to him, "Follow me.""

John 2:2, "and Jesus and his disciples had also been invited to the wedding."

John 2:12, "After this he went down to Capernaum with his mother and brothers and his disciples. There they stayed for a few days."

John 3:22, "After this, Jesus and his disciples went out into the Judean countryside, where he spent some time with them, and baptized."

John 6:3, "Then Jesus went up on a mountainside and sat down with his disciples."

John 11:54, "Therefore Jesus no longer moved about publicly among the Jews. Instead he withdrew to a region near the desert, to a village called Ephraim, where he stayed with his disciples."

John 18:1, "When he had finished praying, Jesus left with his disciples and crossed the Kidron Valley. On the other side there was an olive grove, and he and his disciples went into it."

John 18:2, "Now Judas, who betrayed him, knew the place, because Jesus had often met there with his disciples.

JESUS TEACHES THE TWELVE.

Matthew 5:1-2, "[1]Now when he saw the crowds, he went up on a mountainside and sat down. His disciples came to him, [2] and he began to teach them, saying:"

Matthew 13: 36-37, "[36]Then he left the crowd and went into the house. His disciples came to him and said, "Explain to us the parable of the weeds in the field." [37] He answered..."

Mark 4:10-11, "When he was alone, the Twelve and the others around him asked him about the parables. [11] He told them..."

Mark 8 :27, "Jesus and his disciples went on to the villages around Caesarea Philippi. On the way he asked them, "Who do people say I am?"

Mark 9:35, "Sitting down, Jesus called the Twelve and said, "If anyone wants to be first, he must be the very last, and the servant of all."

Mark 10:13-14, "People were bringing little children to Jesus to have him touch them, but the disciples rebuked them. [14] When Jesus saw this, he was indignant."

Mark 10:28-29, "Peter said to him, "We have left everything to follow you!" [29] "I tell you the truth," Jesus replied."

Mark 10:32, "They were on their way up to Jerusalem, with Jesus leading the way, and the disciples were astonished, while those who followed were afraid. Again he took the Twelve aside and told them what was going to happen to him."

Mark 10:41-42, "When the ten heard about this, they became indignant with James and John. [42] Jesus called them together and said....."

Mark 12:43, "Calling his disciples to him, Jesus said, "I tell you the truth, this poor widow has put more into the treasury than all the others."

Mark 14:12, "On the first day of the Feast of Unleavened Bread, when it was customary to sacrifice the Passover lamb, Jesus' disciples asked him, "Where do you want us to go and make preparations for you to eat the Passover?"

Luke 6:20, "Looking at his disciples, he said: "Blessed are you who are poor, for yours is the kingdom of God."

Luke 10:23, "Then he turned to his disciples and said privately, "Blessed are the eyes that see what you see."

Luke 12:1, "Meanwhile, when a crowd of many thousands had gathered, so that they were trampling on one another, Jesus began to speak first to his disciples, saying:....."

Luke 16:1, "Jesus told his disciples: "There was a rich man whose manager was accused of wasting his possessions."

Luke 18:28-29, "Peter said to him, "We have left all we had to follow you!" ^{29} "I tell you the truth," Jesus said to them."

John 1:43, "The next day Jesus decided to leave for Galilee. Finding Philip, he said to him, "Follow me."

JESUS GIVES INSTRUCTION TO THE TWELVE

Matthew 11:1, "After Jesus had finished instructing his twelve disciples, he went on from there to teach and preach in the towns of Galilee."

Mark 3:9, "Because of the crowd he told his disciples to have a small boat ready for him, to keep the people from crowding him."

Mark 6:7-8, "Calling the Twelve to him, he sent them out two by two and gave them authority over evil spirits. 8 These were his instructions....."

Mark 8:1, "During those days another large

crowd gathered. Since they had nothing to eat, Jesus called his disciples to him and said,….."

Matthew 10:1-5, "He called his twelve disciples to him and gave them authority to drive out evil spirits and to heal every disease and sickness. [2] These are the names of the twelve apostles: first, Simon (who is called Peter) and his brother Andrew; James son of Zebedee, his brother John; [3] Philip and Bartholomew; Thomas and Matthew the tax collector; James son of Alphaeus, and Thaddaeus; [4] Simon the Zealot and Judas Iscariot, who betrayed him. [5] These twelve Jesus sent out with the following instructions:….."

Matthew 14:19, "And he directed the people to sit down on the grass. Taking the five loaves and the two fish and looking up to heaven, he gave thanks and broke the loaves. Then he gave them to the disciples, and the disciples gave them to the people."

Luke 8:22, "One day Jesus said to his disciples, "Let's go over to the other side of the lake." So they got into a boat and set out."

John 11:7, "Then he said to his disciples, "Let us go back to Judea.""

JESUS PRAYS WITH THE TWELVE

Luke 9:18, "Once when Jesus was praying in private and his disciples were with him, he asked them, "Who do the crowds say I am?"

Luke 11:1-2, "¹One day Jesus was praying in a certain place. When he finished, one of his disciples said to him, "Lord, teach us to pray, just as John taught his disciples." ² He said to them, "When you pray, say:....."

Luke 22:39-40, "³⁹Jesus went out as usual to the Mount of Olives, and his disciples followed him. ⁴⁰ On reaching the place, he said to them, "Pray that you will not fall into temptation."

John 17:6-19, "⁶(Jesus Prays for His Disciples) "I have revealed you to those whom you gave me out of the world. They were yours; you gave them to me and they have obeyed your word. ⁷ Now they know that everything you have given me comes from you. ⁸ For I gave them the words you gave me and they accepted them. They knew with certainty that I came from you, and they believed that you sent me. ⁹ I pray for them. I am not praying for the world, but for those you have given me, for they are yours. ¹⁰ All I have is yours, and all you have is mine. And glory has come to me through them. ¹¹ I will remain in the world no longer, but they are still in the world, and I am coming to you. Holy Father, protect them by the power of your name–the name you gave me–so that they may be one as we are one. ¹² While I was with them, I protected them and kept them safe by that name you gave me. None has been lost except the one doomed to destruction so that Scripture would be fulfilled. ¹³ "I am coming to you now, but I say these things while I am still in the world, so that they may have the full measure of my joy within them. ¹⁴ I have given them your word and the world has hated them, for they are not of the world any more than I am of the world. ¹⁵ My prayer is not that you take them out of the world but that you protect them from the evil one. ¹⁶ They are not of the world, even as I am not of it. ¹⁷ Sanctify them by the truth; your word is truth. ¹⁸ As you sent me into the world, I have sent them into the world. ¹⁹ For them I sanctify myself, that they too may be truly sanctified."

JESUS EATS WITH THE TWELVE

Mark 2:15, "While Jesus was having dinner at Levi's house, many tax collectors and "sinners" were eating with him and his disciples, for there were many who followed him."

Mark 3:20, "Then Jesus entered a house, and again a crowd gathered, so that he and his disciples were not even able to eat."

Luke 6:1, "One Sabbath Jesus was going through the grain fields, and his disciples began to pick some heads of grain, rub them in their hands and eat the kernels."

JESUS WITH THE THREE

Mark 5:37, "He did not let anyone follow him except Peter, James and John the brother of James."

Mark 9:2, "After six days Jesus took Peter,

James and John with him and led them up a high mountain, where they were all alone. There he was transfigured before them."

Mark 13:3, "As Jesus was sitting on the Mount of Olives opposite the temple, Peter, James, John and Andrew asked him privately,....."

Mark 14:33, "He took Peter, James and John along with him, and he began to be deeply distressed and troubled."

Luke 8:51, "When he arrived at the house of Jairus, he did not let anyone go in with him except Peter, John and James, and the child's father and mother."

Luke 22:8, "Jesus sent Peter and John, saying, "Go and make preparations for us to eat the Passover."

John 21:15, "When they had finished eating, Jesus said to Simon Peter, "Simon son of John, do you truly love me more than these?" "Yes, Lord," he said, "you know that I love you." Jesus said, "Feed my lambs."

Mark 6:7-13, "[7]Calling the Twelve to him, he sent them out two by two and gave them authority over evil spirits. [8] These were his instructions: "Take nothing for the journey except a staff–no bread, no bag, no money in your belts. [9] Wear sandals but not an extra tunic. [10] Whenever you enter a house, stay there until you leave that town. [11] And if any place will not welcome you or listen to you, shake the dust off your feet when you leave, as a testimony against them." [12] They went out and preached that people should repent. [13] They drove out many demons and anointed many sick people with oil and healed them."

Mark 6:30, "The apostles gathered around Jesus and reported to him all they had done and taught."

Matthew 10:1, "He called his twelve disciples to him and gave them authority to drive out evil spirits and to heal every disease and sickness."

Luke 9:6, "So they set out and went from village to village, preaching the gospel and healing people everywhere."

Luke 9:10, "When the apostles returned, they reported to Jesus what they had done. Then he took them with him and they withdrew by themselves to a town called Bethsaida."

JESUS SENDS OUT 72

Luke 10:1-4, "[1]After this the Lord appointed seventy-two others and sent them two by two ahead of him to every town and place where he was about to go. [2] He told them, "The harvest is plentiful, but the workers are few. Ask the Lord of the harvest, therefore, to send out workers into his harvest field. [3] Go! I am sending you out like lambs among wolves. [4] Do not take a purse or bag or sandals; and do not greet anyone on the road."

CHECK THE WEIGHT AGAIN
PLEASE.

THE **WEIGHT** OF
PREACHING 13
vs
DISCIPLESHIP 61

Hold up there old boy. Are you telling me that Jesus spent almost 5 times more with His disciples training and teaching them, than He did preaching to the people. (Me talking) Yep, that's the way the ball bounces. Then why in Heaven's name do we spend all our time in the pulpit and prepping for Sunday sermons? (Me talking) Don't know, why you do this? A little disclaimer here. Churches are a definite part of God's plan. Corporate worship, prayer, fellowship and the Word are solid pillars to the body of Christ. I have no interest in degrading pillars of God's house. I do believe that the plan to build the house of God is needing a second touch to see clearly once again. That plan is to go back to the basics and do what Jesus did.

Some ministers have the gifts and talents to move church people forward into growth from the pulpit. I would pray that many more would have this ability.

I will add that they, by spiritual nature, understand the building of men and transmit that to others. In this process the church grows. This is a very natural process. The church will be alive and active and new people will be brought in by the church folks. Sheep produce sheep. The pastor is also spending much time with a handful of disciples. He might even have an Apostles calling in His gifts.

In Ephesians 4:11-16, "[11]It was he who gave some to be apostles, some to be prophets, some to be evangelists, and some to be pastors and teachers, [12] to prepare God's people for works of service, so that the body of Christ may be built up [13] until we all reach unity in the faith and in the knowledge of the Son of God and become mature, attaining to the whole measure of the fullness of Christ. [14] Then we will no longer be infants, tossed back and forth by the waves, and blown here and there by every wind of teaching and by the cunning and craftiness of men in their deceitful scheming. [15] Instead, speaking the truth in love, we will in all things grow up into him who is the Head, that is, Christ. [16] From him the whole body, joined and held together by every supporting ligament, grows and builds itself up in love, as each part does its work."

DISCIPLESHIP is the process of helping people get to maturity in the body of Christ. A mature Christian is one who can feed themselves spiritually, share the faith at the drop of a hat, understands that we are in a war of souls, and have Christ at the forefront of their mind. These are just a few basics to think about.

So we have 5 called gifts to the church here. All have been commissioned with a purpose. These come in different levels and shades of power. There is a spiritual order of authority to this structure. Also to note, some have 5 talents, some 2, and some 1. These gifts should blend and work together to support the body. That means there are people in your church that can help with the leadership and discipleship to cause maturity to take place. The strength of your gifts, talents, and abilities are measured by your time and effort involved.

I might add that this does not have much to do with the two hours you spend on Sunday service. Discipleship is a 24/7 process. It is a lifestyle.

Jesus wants us to grow in, works of service, unity in the body, knowledge of the Lord, and become mature. When Jesus told us to be the salt and light to the world, He meant for us to be that where we spend our life and time. Home, work, and community. Most of our growth will take place at night in our home, and at work for 8 hours a day. Sunday church is minor, compared to the rest of the week.

Your gifts, talents, and abilities are given to you to win souls. Take advantage of that.

COMMISSION TO THE CALLED ONE

Instead of the wonderful 52 sermons we try to create year after year, I wonder if we can test what we are doing by the commission we were called to do.

Jesus commissioned the leadership to know the people within the body they are serving. He expects us to train them up, and to be built into a spiritual house. 1 Peter 2:4-5, "[4]As you come to him, the living Stone—rejected by men but chosen by God and precious to him— [5] you also, like living stones, are being built into a spiritual house to be a holy priesthood, offering spiritual sacrifices acceptable to God through Jesus Christ."

Being a house builder myself, when I nail a board in place it is still there years later. We are also being built into a spiritual house to stay.

We are all to be a holy priesthood, offering spiritual sacrifice which will be pleasing to our God. He is worthy of this.

Some of the Lord's disciples did not think this was the way to go. Read John 6:66, "From this time on many of his disciples turned back and no longer followed him." Strange, 666, does that mean something? Interesting how some numbers fit in.

Let's look at some of the teachings we are to minister on.

In Ephesians 4:12, "to prepare God's people for works of service...."

The question here, can you tell me what each person is doing outside the 2 hour window that you get to see them, is doing for the kingdom of God?

Are they sharing the Lord at work, or with a neighbor? Did they visit the sick, or go to the jail? Are they building something in the garage to give away at Christmas to the kids that don't have much? Did they help with the yard work for their sick boss or neighbor? Did they volunteer at the food bank? Did they ask you if you needed any help at the church building? There is only about 10,000 more things I could ask here.

The point is that God has prepared work for all of us to do. Our ministry as leaders is to help people find their personal ministry gifts, talents and calls.

Ephesians 2:10, "For we are God's workmanship, created in Christ Jesus to do good works, which God prepared in advance for us to do."

Ephesians 4:13, "until we all reach unity in the faith and in the knowledge of the Son of God and become mature...."

A major goal is to bring unity of faith into the lives of the believers. Unity is the one force that makes the devil run for cover. In Philippians 1:27-28, "[27]Whatever happens, conduct yourselves in a manner worthy of the gospel of Christ. Then, whether I come and see you or only hear about you in my absence, I will know that you stand firm in one spirit, contending as one man for the faith of the gospel [28] without being frightened in any way by those who oppose you. This is a sign to them that they will be destroyed, but that you will be saved—and that by God."

In Ephesians 4:3-6, "[3]Make every effort to keep the unity of the Spirit through the bond of peace. [4] There is one body and one Spirit—just as you were called to one hope when you were called — [5] one Lord, one faith, one baptism; [6] one God and Father of all, who is over all and through all and in all."

Unity comes through discipleship, when we help people go from milk to meat. One on one love and prayer.

Unity also comes through the mantle or cloak of humility, given by the Holy Spirit.

Unity comes as we learn to yield to the voice of Jesus sharing with us.

Ephesians 4:13 B, "...attaining to the whole measure of the fullness of Christ."

KNOWLEDGE OF THE SON OF GOD.

This is a personal relationship, between you and the Lord, as you share the faith with others.

Philemon 1:6, "I pray that you may be active in sharing your faith, so that you will have a full understanding of every good thing we have in Christ."

2 Peter 1:2, "Grace and peace be yours in abundance through the knowledge of God and of Jesus our Lord."

Colossians 2:2-3, "²My purpose is that they may be encouraged in heart and united in love, so that they may have the full riches of complete understanding, in order that they may know the mystery of God, namely, Christ, ³ in whom are hidden all the treasures of wisdom and knowledge."

If you don't or won't share Christ,
and be a witness for Him,
you will never have an understanding or
a personal relationship with Him!

I refer to Matthew 7:21-23, "²¹Not everyone who says to me, 'Lord, Lord,' will enter the kingdom of heaven, but only he who does the will of my Father who is in heaven. ²² Many will say to me on that day, 'Lord, Lord, did we not prophesy in your name, and in your name drive out demons and perform many miracles?' ²³ Then I will tell them plainly, 'I never knew you. Away from me, you evildoers!'"

> ## GOD'S WILL IS THAT
> ## ALL MEN BE SAVED.
>
> ## JESUS DIED SO THAT
> ## MAN COULD BE SAVED.
>
> ## THE HOLY SPIRIT IS HERE SO THAT
> ## MAN CAN BE SAVED.

I repeat... The spearhead to our faith is when I said Lord come into my heart. I received the heartbeat of God for souls, souls, soul!! Now everybody I meet is a potential disciple of Christ.

Training is life to a new believer. Help these caterpillars to become butterflies. Check your people with an EKG, to see if there is a good heartbeat. (attaining to the whole measure of the fullness of Christ.)

Understanding Christ and the plan that God has given us to do, is very simplistic. 1 Corinthians 2:6-16, "[6]We do, however, speak a message of wisdom among the mature, but not the wisdom of this age or of the rulers of this age, who are coming to nothing. [7] No, we speak of God's secret wisdom, a wisdom that has been hidden and that God destined for our glory before time began. [8] None of the rulers of this age understood it, for if they had, they would not have crucified the Lord of glory. [9] However, as it is written: "No eye has seen, no ear has heard, no mind has conceived what

God has prepared for those who love him"–[10] but God has revealed it to us by his Spirit. The Spirit searches all things, even the deep things of God. [11] For who among men knows the thoughts of a man except the man's spirit within him? In the same way no one knows the thoughts of God except the Spirit of God. [12] We have not received the spirit of the world but the Spirit who is from God, that we may understand what God has freely given us. [13] This is what we speak, not in words taught us by human wisdom but in words taught by the Spirit, expressing spiritual truths in spiritual words. [14] The man without the Spirit does not accept the things that come from the Spirit of God, for they are foolishness to him, and he cannot understand them, because they are spiritually discerned. [15] The spiritual man makes judgments about all things, but he himself is not subject to any man's judgment: [16] "For who has known the mind of the Lord that he may instruct him?" But we have the mind of Christ."

There it is, we have the mind of Christ. We have the Holy Spirit living within. The word or the principles of the Lord are imprinted on our heart and mind. The understanding of the Lord comes to us as we share the faith. And this drives us to want to learn more, to read more of the Word, and to fellowship with the Saints, and pray to and praise the Lord.

We understand that there is either the Lordship of the Lord or the devil, and that you can only serve one at a time. When we meet a new person, we are in one of two modes. Either a ministry mode or a fellowship mode. You will know the difference as your spiritual antennas sense their spirits.

We will always know how to respond to any situation, because we simply ask our self, What Would Jesus Do? WWJD?

Are work in the Lord will be to build relationships, by growing the Fruit of the Spirit, and learning how to use our mistakes as stairways, instead of stumbling blocks.

We will master our homes in Christian living, and be examples to others. In this way we can master the work place and the world.

COMMISSION TO THE CALLED ONES

As Paul puts it is his words. Philippians 3:7-16, "[7]But whatever was to my profit I now consider loss for the sake of Christ. [8] What is more, I consider everything a loss compared to the surpassing greatness of knowing Christ Jesus my Lord, for whose sake I have lost all things. I consider them rubbish, that I may gain Christ [9] and be found in him, not having a righteousness of my own that comes from the law, but that which is through faith in Christ–the righteousness that comes from God and is by faith. [10] I want to know Christ and the power of his resurrection and the fellowship of sharing in his sufferings, becoming like him in his death, [11] and so, somehow, to attain to the resurrection from the dead. Pressing on Toward the Goal [12] Not that I have already obtained all this, or have already been made perfect, but I press on to take hold of that for which Christ Jesus took hold of me. [13] Brothers, I do not consider myself yet to have taken hold of it. But one thing I do: Forgetting what is behind and straining toward what is ahead, [14] I press on toward the goal to win the prize for which God has called me heavenward in Christ Jesus. [15] All of us who are mature should take such a view of things. And if on some point you think differently, that too God will make clear to you. [16] Only let us live up to what we have already attained."

Ya gotta love Paul. It seems that we try to be politically correct and not offend the people today. It feels like we are stepping on eggs shells. Honesty and sincerity, with all the aid of the Fruit of the Spirit it is enough. People are looking for truth today, not a mask. We need to preach the truth now. John 8:31-32, "[31]To the Jews who had believed him, Jesus said, "If you hold to my teaching, you are really my disciples. [32] Then you will know the truth, and the truth will set you free."

THE NEWBIES

Ephesians 4:14-16, "[14]Then we will no longer be infants, tossed back and forth by the waves, and blown here and there by every wind of teaching and by the cunning and craftiness of men in their deceitful scheming. [15] Instead, speaking the truth in love, we will in all things grow up into him who is the Head, that is, Christ. [16] From him the whole body, joined and held together by every supporting ligament, grows and builds itself up in love, as each part does its work."

Your greatest area of activity is right here. The attitude of us 4 and no more is bad news. I can't tell you how to do your service, but if it does not catch the attention of the newbies, you will probably not grow a church. A major part of the service needs to be devoted to the newbies.

Fellowship on Sunday has taken a seat in the back of the bus. Fellowship today is staring at the back of someone's head in front of you.

We come in and shake a hand or two and then sit and wait for the music. Once the sermon is over we walk out and shake the Pastor's hand, get in the car and go home. Now that is some fellowship.

When do we get to know the person in front of us, or behind us? Do we even know how to pray for the one over on the other side of the room? Who is having a real struggle today? Who could use a friend?   Can we sing happy birthday to someone, or say happy anniversary? Who just got out of the hospital and needs a little help, or where is old Joe, did he die?   Fellowship is very much needed for a healthy church to grow.   Someone say, amen!

We did a simple thing in one church we pastored. The youth group put on a lunch every Sunday for all to come and join. Either a soup or salad one Sunday. Then sandwiches, then tacos, and so forth.

Games were on the table and people would come eat, talk, and play games. We pastored there a little over 5 years. We never held a service in those 5 years of which we did at least 3 services a week, where at least 1 soul was saved at every service. I might add that the youth only charged a little bit for their services, which helped support them and their camp needs.

The entire church was not afraid to do street ministry, door to door ministry, or pass out tracks at the fair.   That's also why so many souls were brought into the Kingdom of God.

Each member was trained up in love, to do his part of the work of ministry.

DISCIPLESHIP IS HARD WORK

There is a cost to being a disciple of Jesus our Lord.

Matthew 10:37-39, "[37]Anyone who loves his father or mother more than me is not worthy of me; anyone who loves his son or daughter more than me is not worthy of me; [38] and anyone who does not take his cross and follow me is not worthy of me. [39] Whoever finds his life will lose it, and whoever loses his life for my sake will find it."

Here is the question to understanding this verse. Who is number one in your heart and life?

Luke 14:25-27, "²⁵Large crowds were traveling with Jesus, and turning to them he said: ²⁶ "If anyone comes to me and does not hate his father and mother, his wife and children, his brothers and sisters–yes, even his own life–he cannot be my disciple. ²⁷ And anyone who does not carry his cross and follow me cannot be my disciple."

It's about the priority of Lordship. Jesus first, even over your wants or opinions. His will is first over your spouse and family. We need to hate, or love less everything compared to His love first. He is looking for a very personal and close relationship with you, no holds barred.

When it comes to Lordship, it's my way or the highway. Spiritually speaking of course. We really need to die to self, or we are just spitting in the wind.

Luke 14:28-35, "²⁸Suppose one of you wants to build a tower. Will he not first sit down and estimate the cost to see if he has enough money to complete it? ²⁹ For if he lays the foundation and is not able to finish it, everyone who sees it will ridicule him, ³⁰ saying, 'This fellow began to build and was not able to finish.' ³¹ "Or suppose a king is about to go to war against another king. Will he not first sit down and consider whether he is able with ten thousand men to oppose the one coming against him with twenty thousand? ³² If he is not able, he will send a delegation while the other is still a long way off and will ask for terms of peace. ^{33} In the same way, any of you who does not give up everything he has cannot be my disciple. ^{34} "Salt is good, but if it loses its saltiness, how can it be made salty again? ^{35} It is fit neither for the soil nor for the manure pile; it is thrown out. "He who has ears to hear, let him hear."

Do you really think that you can put on the gloves, and get into the ring and duke it out with the King of Kings? Our pea brains and opinions are no match against the Master. Give them up and die to self.

Luke 9:57-62, "^{57}As they were walking along the road, a man said to him, "I will follow you wherever you go." ^{58} Jesus replied, "Foxes have holes and birds of the air have nests, but the Son of Man has no place to lay his head." ^{59} He said to another man, "Follow me." But the man replied, "Lord, first let me go and bury my father." ^{60} Jesus said to him, "Let the dead bury their own dead, but you go and proclaim the kingdom of God." ^{61} Still another said, "I will follow you, Lord; but first let me go back and say goodbye to my family." ^{62} Jesus replied, "No one who puts his hand to the plow and looks back is fit for service in the kingdom of God."

Foxes have holes...Jesus was telling this man that you can't depend on your self and your stuff.

Let me bury my father...Jesus was telling him now is your time, and your excuses to wait for your father to die and get his money to live on will be too late.

Go back and say goodbye...Jesus says, so you want to party first for a few more days, I got it. Tradition for a journey was a party given for several days.

When people wanted to come on their terms, Jesus was not interested in them. Party on.

Today, what does it look like if you carry the cross? It is the present tense fruit of the spirit, living in us. We are all made with body, soul and spirit. Our spirit lives in the present tense, coupled with the holy fruit that transmits around us (which is our cross to bear) by our spirit. That present tense fruit (the cross) is being received or pick up by nonbelievers and is knocking at the door of their hearts. So pick up your cross and carry it. Be fruitful.

DISCIPLESHIP IS HARD WORK

Programs have taken over in the place of Discipleship. Programs consist of Sunday school teaching books, midweek Bible study of some book, and youth groups love games and hot music. I'm not trying to be critical here, I'm making a prophetic point. Carried along by the Spirit in love of course.

Some may not agree with this and throw this book away. That's OK with me. I'm just a messenger.

The point is that Discipleship is a lifestyle. I read the Bible and talk to the Lord, and prepare myself daily. I am a walking Bible. I'm the only Bible some people will ever read. This is my life in the Lord.

When I talk to anyone, anywhere, the Bible comes through loud and clear. I don't wear a bumper sticker on my tail feathers, or sound a trumpet when I approach people. I simply have my spiritual antennas up and polished, sensing whether they are serving God or satan. If they are serving God, I'm in a fellowship mode and encourage them all I can in that brief moment in time. If they are serving Satan, I go into ministry mode and look for an opportunity to share the Lord and my testimony.

I look for opportunities to share. When the doors shut on the elevator, no one is going anywhere. I say, I suppose you are wondering why I've called this meeting today? It's to tell you that Jesus is alive and well, and wants to invite you all to heaven. Anybody want to keep going up?

It takes gifts and experience to pull this off, to where people enjoy the approach of this kind of a witness. I could be a cartoon character at times.

Taking people under your wing so to speak, is a lot of work. That's why the church has stopped doing it in the original form. To do discipling requires hours of your life given to another. You will study for them, serve them, help them get out of trouble, and correct them. You'll need to pray for them, visit them, teach them, and carry the cross for them. Your sacrifice will pay off, and blessings will shower you from above. Your life will take on a purpose as never before. Your relationship with the Lord will grow leaps and bounds.

It's also the most enjoyable life you can have. It is a lifestyle, not a program. You learn to roll with this style. It does not take anything away from you, it brings blessings to your life. Right now I have hundreds of spiritual children, grandchildren, and great grandchildren all over the planet. Most of them I do not even know.

DISCIPLESHIP IS HARD WORK

If we carry the cross, we won't have time to pick up sin.

A few scriptures:

Luke 14:27, "And anyone who does not carry his cross and follow me cannot be my disciple."

Luke 14:33, "In the same way, any of you who does not give up everything he has cannot be my disciple."

Luke 9:23, "Then he said to them all: "If anyone would come after me, he must deny himself and take up his cross daily and follow me."

John 8:31-32, "[31]To the Jews who had believed him, Jesus said, "If you hold to my teaching, you are really my disciples. [32] Then you will know the truth, and the truth will set you."

Matthew 10:38-39, "and anyone who does not take his cross and follow me is not worthy of me. [39] Whoever finds his life will lose it, and whoever loses his life for my sake will find it."

Jesus is more interested in winning 100% of you than you winning 100% of the world. He is not harsh at all in these verses. He knows mans heart, and He knew when men were just making excuses.

When you put your hand to the plow, don't look back. If you do, your plow line will not be straight and then people will laugh at you. It will be an embarrassment to all involved. In other words, Jesus will get a black eye.

Philippians 3:17-21, "[17]Join with others in following my example, brothers, and take note of those who live according to the pattern we gave you. [18] For, as I have often told you before and now say again even with tears, many live as enemies of the cross of Christ. [19] Their destiny is destruction, their god is their stomach, and their glory is in their shame. Their mind is on earthly things. [20] But our citizenship is in heaven. And we eagerly await a Savior from there, the Lord Jesus Christ, [21] who, by the power that enables him to bring everything under his control, will transform our lowly bodies so that they will be like his glorious body."

Hebrew 4:4-6, "[4]It is impossible for those who have once been enlightened, who have tasted the heavenly gift, who have shared in the Holy Spirit, [5] who have tasted the goodness of the word of God and the powers of the coming age, [6] if they fall away, to be brought back to repentance, because to their loss they are crucifying the Son of God all over again and subjecting him to public disgrace." (BLACK EYE)

DISCIPLESHIP IS HARD WORK

Paul told us in Philippians 4:9, "Whatever you have learned or received or heard from me, or seen in me–put it into practice. And the God of peace will be with you."

Paul was not arrogant when he made this statement. This statement is one that should be made by all mature Christians. Our lifestyles should reflect the love of Jesus Himself. People around us should be able to tell that there is a difference between us and the world.

1 Corinthians 11:1, "Follow my example, as I follow the example of Christ."

Hebrew 3:1, "Therefore, holy brothers, who share in the heavenly calling, fix your thoughts on

Jesus, the apostle and high priest whom we confess."

Christ is the center focus of our lives. There is room for everything else that's important, when He is on center stage. Your life will only improve when you follow and fix your eyes on Him.

Philippians 3:17, "Join with others in following my example, brothers, and take note of those who live according to the pattern we gave you."

The only pattern we share is Jesus Christ Himself. He is what we focus on. He is what people come to see. That's why He is on our center stage of life. Now when people of the world see and recognize the difference in you, tell them what Paul said, "Whatever you have learned or received or heard from me, or seen in me–put it into practice. And the God of peace will be with you."

You will not be bragging, you will just be in love with Jesus. We call this our spiritual act of worship.

Romans 12:1-2, "[1]Therefore, I urge you, brothers, in view of God's mercy, to offer your bodies as living sacrifices, holy and pleasing to God–this is your spiritual act of worship. [2] Do not conform any longer to the pattern of this world, but be transformed by the renewing of your mind. Then you will be able to test and approve what God's will is–his good, pleasing and perfect will." (God's will the Heartbeat).

Simple isn't it. Told you so. KISS. Keep It Simple Sweetheart.

NEED A LEADER
FOURTEEN THINGS TO LOOK FOR IN A LEADER

1. Are they excited, enthusiastic, full of joy?

2. Are they diligent, want to do a job right?

3. Do they accept responsibility willingly?

4. Do they show a fruitful personality?

5. Are they teachable, flexible, adjustable?

6. Do they adhere to the Great Commands to love?

7. Do they have a servant's heart, show humility?

8. Do people follow them?

9. Are they loyal to friends?

10. Can they communicate?

11. Do they love God's Word?

12. Do they love the body of Christ?

13. Do they love the anointing as they share God's Word?

14. Do they share the heartbeat of lost souls?

TWELVE STEPS TO DISCIPLESHIP

1. Find a good example.
2. Develop a relationship with them.
3. Make a promise to submit and learn.
4. Learn to deny yourself.
5. Pick up your cross.
6. Be teachable.
7. Be Faithful to your leaders and to the Lord.
8. Be obedient to authority.
9. Work under authority.
10. Follow assignments.
11. Let the leadership recognize your gifts and talents.
12. Prepare to be released for ministry.

49747515R00100

Made in the USA
Columbia, SC
26 January 2019